The Color of God's Grace

By Claudia Noble

Dedicated with love to my husband

Acknowledgments

This book began when I was sitting on a plane, of course. We were grounded for about an hour and I texted my friend Marsha that I was getting desperate because I didn't have anything to read. Thus started the game of Marsha sending me writing prompts. I whipped up a few stories and shared them with friends; they liked them, and I decided it was time to jump back into my on again-off again writing career. I had the courage at last to tell this story through a full length book.

It sounds like such a cliche, but it's true, I couldn't have done it without the help of my friends. Each time someone said they had been touched by a little passage I had written, or whenever someone said, "You've captured that exactly," my normally low confidence level got a little boost. I want to thank my local writer friends, especially Laurie Lunsford and Sharon Davy, for their advice and encouragement. My editor, Judy Martin Urban, is responsible for cutting out all those commas and unnecessary words I seem to love to include. Betty Millspaugh McBride, thank you for making me feel like I had a personal cheerleader! And credit and love go out to my friends at the Yorktown Community Library. They are all great there, but it's Laurie Hogue and Lisa Hoover in particular who have to listen to me jabber on when I get excited about something, and then help me when my limited computer skills have me crying out for rescue.

Of course I thank my family, for living through all of this with me, and I thank my vast HAE family, many I have met, and many I have not, who daily live with the extremely challenging condition, Hereditary Angioedema. I love you all!

To learn more about Hereditary Angioedema, please visit www.haea.org.

For info on obtaining the inspiring documentary about HAE, "Special Blood", see www.specialblood.com

Chapter 1

Wondering

Forward, back, forward, back. I pushed and drug my feet through the soft gray dirt under my swing that hung from our old catalpa tree. I spent so many hours there, pondering, wondering. It seems that even at five years old I was trying to figure out who I was. There was a tall, elegant, brick house just down my street, always in my line of vision from the swing, and I spent a lot of time wishing I was a movie star who lived there. Or at least somebody important and glamorous.

When did it happen? When did I first feel that color had left my life and how had it happened? I'd carried inside of me a memory of some elevated sense of happiness, in a place where everything was warm and beautiful. It had indescribable color, almost as if someone had painted the world in thick, tangible strokes of endless hues. This colorful world seemed to be gone now, but how? Why?

I really don't believe I can say it was lost through some terrible childhood event.

I grew up with a reasonably comfortable life, in an average small Midwest city. We did not struggle financially; my father was a security guard at the large Chevrolet plant in town. My sisters and I knew we were loved. There was a lot of laughter, especially in late night conversations between Mother and her three girls, my two older sisters and myself.

There was often some tension from one thing, and that was my father's drinking. He was a good man. He certainly didn't act out in a mean way when drinking, but it *was* a big thing in our family. Mostly, I remember the worry and anxiety it caused my mother, as she tried to cover up for him when he couldn't go to work, or tried to keep the "secret" from her mother-in-law, who lived in a small house just behind us.

It probably wasn't a secret. I later learned that my father's own father had his own battles with alcohol and depression. Maybe my dad was trying to forget some painful memories from his childhood. Maybe there was a chemical predisposition, if not to alcoholism, at least to a tendency towards depression.

Unfortunately, I was to go through many times of depression myself in the years to come. Maybe it was even starting back then, in those days of sitting in my swing and feeling that happiness was somehow just out of my reach.

Overall, though, my growing up years were marked by the security and privilege that a working-class family could enjoy in the 1950's and '60's. I had good friends. We played baseball in the field at the nearby park. We rode bikes everywhere.

We could go to the local Flagpole restaurant and buy a dish of raspberry sherbet for a quarter or ride to the gas station and spend that quarter on an ice-cold Dr. Pepper. In the winters there was sledding and snowman building and cold walks to school with my best friend, Cynthia.

I kept my "something's missing" feelings to myself, but I was always wondering, trying to grasp the memory of a time when I thought life was painted in shining, brilliant colors, not these pale, dreary tints of gray. How could I get back to that time? Did it have something to do with God? People said babies came from God. Maybe I was remembering a better place than this imperfect Earth.

We were Methodists from way back. Well, I later learned that not too many generations back on my mother's side, my ancestors were Quakers, but my childhood memories are of a pretty, Methodist sanctuary with sunlight streaming through the stained-glass windows. There was a stately wooden chair next to the pulpit. It faced towards the congregation. My sister, Janet, told me that was where Jesus sat during the services. This kept me on my good behavior, but one day a visiting minister took the seat and I could hardly keep from yelling out, "You're sitting on Jesus!"

Another memory from that church was playing Baby Jesus in a Christmas play. I was two-and-a-half, I believe, and I remember the spotlight shining down on my face after my sister bundled me up and put me in the manger. I loved singing the old hymns in church. The minister's sermons were always pleasant and comforting, but one Sunday School teacher made me wonder about the joy the Christian life was supposed to bring. Maybe it was just me, but his sour expression while reading scriptures to us and his emphasis on all we had to do to please God planted in my heart worry that I might not be able to measure up.

We were told in Sunday School Jesus was coming back one day and when I tried to imagine it, I decided He would appear in the sky somewhere above the grapevines we had in our backyard. I pictured my parents gathering enough strength and courage to look Him in His face, but I saw myself (and I always thought I would still be a very little girl at the time) turning away in fear, huddled down, covering my own face so I couldn't see all that brightness and holiness. How could I stand before Him?

This mental perception of the fear I would feel lasted a very long time, even to some extent after I felt secure in my Christian faith. Many years later my feelings changed a little when I had a dream. In the dream I was walking down Hoyt Avenue, very near my childhood home. I must have been still thinking of those grapevines. In the sky I saw a distant bright light and it was coming closer and closer. At first, I thought it must be the moon, but then, I saw the face of Jesus inside this shining circle. He looked a lot like the well-known painting, "Head of Christ" my sister had hanging on our bedroom wall, but there was a kind smile on His face, and a look of gentle love. I knew He was coming, and I felt happy. In my dream, and even after awakening, I basked in the relief I felt.

I began to think I could gladly welcome His coming, that it could be a joyous occasion. Before having that dream, I had long been bogged down by my feelings of unworthiness. I hadn't really believed His grace could cover my shortcomings. The kindness I saw on Jesus's face made me begin to believe His love wasn't dependent on how I measured up. It has been a war in my mind, this worrying about my worthiness, for most of my life, but I believe God's grace was working it out for me.

Chapter 2

The Danger

People think a kid can't be depressed and I probably hadn't even heard the word when I was a young, pondering child. So, I reasoned, I must be sick. Not yet aware of the hereditary disease I would later learn I had, I assumed my low energy and sad feelings must mean I was physically ill. Whether I was truly ill or not, it seemed easier to say to my mother, "I'm not feeling well" than to try to explain the vague sadness and anxiety going on inside.

She became frustrated too and often brought out an old favorite saying of mothers everywhere, "Maybe if you eat something you will feel better." (And didn't that backfire on me in my adult years!) But I just couldn't put my feelings into words and many times I know I was thought of as a spoiled, whiny child.

Fear was a big thing with me. Even though there wasn't much to fear in my sheltered, middle-America life, a whole menagerie of scary bears, wolves and gorillas lived inside of me. Maybe that started one night when I truly was ill with some childhood ailment at about age four. I remember trying to sleep on our living room couch. I even remember the horrible taste of the antibiotic I had been given as I lay there with a burning throat and feverish thoughts. Accompanying me that night—

and for many years I could not believe differently—was a devious looking wolf just sitting in the chair across from the couch, waiting to do who knows what to the little kid with the fever. It didn't even make me feel better when I later described the wolf to my mother and his blue overalls and hat tipped her off that I was imagining this from one of my Little Golden books! No, that wolf managed to stick around in my tender little psyche for many years.

If there was danger lurking in our household, I would say it was HAE. Hereditary Angioedema, the hard-to-pronounce (for me, then) condition my mother and my sister, Janet, suffered. I remember so well my sister's cries of pain at night in our dark bedroom. Excruciating abdominal attacks made her and our mother so desperately ill they were often too weak during them to do anything but lie on the bathroom floor, waiting for the next wave of nausea and its aftermath. I felt so sorry for them. I really didn't understand it, and I never expected that HAE would one day change my life so completely.

Hereditary Angioedema is a rare blood disorder. People with HAE (spoken aloud as H-A-E) have a missing, or under-performing, protein in their blood called C1-esterase inhibitor. This protein works to shut off, at the appropriate time, the reaction your immune system creates in response to some kind of trauma. If there is low C1, or defective C1, the reaction continues freely. A bump on the hand, or even say, stepping on a plastic toy while barefoot, might cause a little swelling in the average person's hand or foot. People who have HAE would probably experience uncontrolled swelling. The phrase "vascular permeability" is used to describe what happens. Without C1-inhibitor to keep things stable, fluid is allowed to leak out of the veins and pool in the affected parts of the body, thus the abnormal swelling. This can mean anything from the nuisance of not being able to wear shoes for a day, to a 3 to 5-day siege of pain and vomiting, or even to a life-threatening situation when the airway is involved.

Mostly, I remember my sister's almost weekly attacks and my normally strong mother crying in pain during her bad episodes. I didn't know I had HAE until I was tested at age 12 and found to be positive. It didn't seem to be causing any problem for me, so I have to admit I treated my diagnosis casually.

When I was about 17, my mother was very ill from her HAE and in serious condition in the hospital. I stood at her bedside, so sad to see her struggle and said to her, "I wish it was me." I guess it was just a teenager's way of trying to be strong and sound valiant. I truly did wish I could take her pain away, but she brought me up short when she faintly whispered, "Don't say that. You have your whole life ahead of you."

Shame ran through me as I realized she thought she was dying and that I was wanting to take her place, when I only meant I wanted to trade places with her for the moment. She did make it through that episode, but she later developed severe asthma, and it was terrible watching her struggle daily with this second condition. Although I seemed to have escaped HAE attacks during my teen years, later I looked back and saw where HAE must have been present. For one thing, my menstrual cramps were often much worse than any of my girlfriends'. And after a dental procedure once, I stopped at my employer's place and she didn't know me. I didn't even realize until then how badly my lips and face had swollen. Even if I didn't have full-blown, recognizable HAE attacks, I now know, from trading stories with other patients, that the disorder was probably responsible for much of my childhood malaise and my "feeling sick" times. However, back then, before I had really reached adulthood, HAE mostly seemed to be just waiting in the wings for me.

Chapter 3

Love and Marriage

I met my life's partner in Study Hall. Well, it seems that way since I have so many memories of furtively exchanging notes with the tall, dark-haired guy who sat a few rows over from me in our high school cafeteria during study period. As it turned out, we have been side by side for many decades. And this was in spite of the fact he was first the boyfriend of one of my best friends! I think it turned out the way it was supposed to, though, and she was even in our wedding.

We were married two years after high school. I was working at the city library and he worked for the U.S. Postal Service. There was a draft in those days, but since he worked as a civil servant, he was told he would not be called for at least two years. About ten days before our wedding, I was in my mother's car with her. She noticed I was very upset. "What's the matter?" she asked. "Are you getting cold feet?"

Isn't it grooms that do that? I started to cry and said, "Darrell got his draft notice yesterday!"

Our little storybook life wasn't going to go quite as planned, but March 22nd came and we were wed. After the ceremony, my new husband and I *and* his parents jumped into his '64 Impala to head for the Dayton, OH airport. No, his parents did not fly off to Florida with us. They had gone along in order to drive his beloved Impala home for safekeeping during our honeymoon. They later reported to us they were at first a little mystified by all the honks and waves and smiles they received on the way back home. Then they realized all those passersby thought *they* were the newlyweds merrily tooling down the road in that car covered with red and white streamers and painted-on well wishes.

I stayed in our small apartment and Darrell left for basic training in Fort Knox, KY. After his six weeks of basic training, and then some advanced training, I joined him, since he was told he would be staying at Fort Knox. We spent two beautiful Fall months in Kentucky until, once again we received a surprise. New orders: South Vietnam.

By the time he left for Southeast Asia, we were expecting Baby Number One. Maybe it was young love, blessed ignorance or something else, but I don't feel I worried about my husband too much. My grandfather told me to pray Psalm 91 every night, and I was very thankful for my mother-in-law's constant prayers, because at the end of his overseas tour, my husband came home and held three-month-old Kristin for the first time. We felt we had it all.

That is not to say Kristin came into the world easily. I was so excited to be pregnant and I was ready to take this thing on. Well, my blustering confidence and my cavalier attitude got a jolt of reality with my first pregnancy-related HAE attack. Physical, and even emotional, stress can trigger HAE, and pregnancy certainly brings on a lot of new issues for the body to sort out and address. The changes in my body caused painful, full-blown abdominal swelling episodes, and they became almost a weekly thing for me. In the midst of one of these attacks, while I was twisting back and forth, trying to somehow get away from the waves of pain in my swollen-shut intestines, my mother said to me, "I know. It hurts almost as much as labor pains."

A friend of mine who was a new mother happened to be there too and she took me aside later and said, "Oh Claudia, don't let your mother scare you. Labor does not hurt THAT much!"

Well, I found out the reality of labor, too. I went into premature labor because the placenta began to break up—a partial placental abruption. The next 17 hours passed mostly with the doctor trying to decide whether I would need a C-section or not, but eventually Kristin emerged on her own and I was thrilled, all the pain forgotten.

As baby and I were wheeled out of the delivery room, I noticed the worried looks on the faces of the many family members lining the sides of the hall, peering down at my little bundle. I was playing the proud new mother and I wondered why they were so doleful. Later I was told they thought I was deep in denial, because my little bundle was an ashy blue color, and there I was, beaming. But, my confidence proved merited. My little girl did turn out to be perfect. She had just lost a little oxygen toward the end of the birthing process.

Four years later, Kristin was joined by Ryan, and another year later, by Jeremy. Those were the days I vowed I would never say to a young mother, "I bet you have your hands full," or "Enjoy them while they're little." That is what I heard everywhere I went. Sometimes I just wanted to say to people, "Can't you come up with something original?" I was often frustrated, exhausted, and mentally in a fog, but I loved my three little ones with all my heart.

Even if I got a little exasperated hearing advice from these older women, I did know enough to appreciate those early years. I loved reading to my children. I loved taking them out for neighborhood walks on warm evenings, just before their bedtime. The boys would be dressed in their footie pajamas, and, on cooler evenings, their hooded, zip-up jackets. They rode, paired up, in their double stroller, and Kristin would hold my hand. We would always laugh when we looked back to see our orange and white cat, Casey, hurrying to catch up with us. Casey had her own ritual. She had to walk into every driveway along our path, lie down, roll over twice, then get up and trot along with us until the next driveway.

My mother-in-law had another phrase to add to "Enjoy them while they're young." She would say, "Children walk on your feet when they're little and walk on your heart when they're big." I came to understand that. In their childhood days, even though they were my precious little ones, I wondered when I would ever have time to myself.

I was happy raising a family, but from my perspective of being 20-something or 30-something, being told that someday my children would grow up and be gone didn't mean a lot on my weariest days. My reaction to those assurances was usually, *But I'll be too old to enjoy anything by then*!

God probably had a good laugh at that since He knew there were many enjoyable things in store for me when my little ones were no longer tugging me in three directions, or asking me for a drink, or following me from room to room. I came to understand about children walking on your heart when they are bigger, too. None of them did anything terribly bad, but watching a child stumble through the twists and turns of growing up makes any parent's heart tremble with concern. But, of course, we did get through it all.

Chapter 4

Yes, With All My Heart

"Mommy," Kristin said, "How can you love all three of us with ALL your heart?" She asked because it was one of my favorite things to say to each of them, "I love you with ALL my heart." Kristin is a mom of two now, so I think she must know the answer. To a mother, each child is an amazing blessing she would never have wanted to live without. I am so very thankful for each of mine.

Kristin was my dream come true, a precious little girl of my own. She was also my mother-in-law and father-in-law's dream come true, their first grandchild, on whom they absolutely doted. Kristin made my mother happy by being her first brown-eyed grandchild, which she had wanted for so long!

Kristin grew up loving books, from her first library picture books, to the volumes of Trixie Belden mysteries we bought her when she was a young teen, to the various stacks I know she now keeps by her bedside. She was a very good student; teachers adored her, but it was her kindness and compassion for other kids her age I remember the most about her growing up years. She always listened and encouraged others. She was quick to stand up for a friend. She was also always there for me when I needed her.

When I was going through tests for severe headaches, one day she needed to drive me home from an appointment. I had been sedated for my test, so I apologized to her for being so drowsy, especially since she only had a learner's permit and I should have been paying closer attention to her driving.

"No, that's okay, Mom," she said, "I kind of like you this way when I'm driving."

Kristin and I went through a lot together. One of the things was she had to endure going to college at the same time as her mom. In my late 30s, I decided I was going to get that college degree I had not pursued at the traditional age of 18 or so. I loved it—the studying, the reading, the writing, even all the walking across campus, going from class to class. I did receive my degree, but not within the normal four years, so I was still taking classes when it was time for Kristin to start, at the same university. We overlapped about a year.

Fortunately, I had always gotten along well with Kristin's friends, and her new friends in college didn't mind my tagging along once in a while. It gave me a fun taste of what I otherwise would have missed, not going to college at the traditional age. There was even a mother-daughter night, when moms got to stay overnight in their daughters' dorm rooms. One of the activities in her dorm was playing a form of the old TV show, "The Newlywed Game." This version had mothers and daughters trying to match each others' answers to various questions. Kristin and I went into it knowing we

20

would win it, because we knew each other so well. And we won. Poor Kristin just couldn't escape her mother in those days.

As for the outcome of our respective educations, I have used mine mostly by doing freelance writing through the years, as well as substitute teaching in all grades; Kristin has made her career in public libraries. I am proud of her. She has been great in all of her roles: puppeteer for children's library programs (the puppet shows were actually televised), manager and sole employee of a tiny branch library in Tennessee, an information specialist and a teacher of genealogy classes.

Ryan, our second child, was born a serious little boy. When he was ten months old, I took him for swimming lessons at the YWCA. I remember the instructor had me just kind of toss Ryan to him in the water. I was standing in the water and the instructor was only a few yards away. The idea, evidently, was that instinct would take over and Ryan would automatically start to swim. He did make it to the young teacher, but of course his head had gone under water and he ingested several big gulps. The instructor quickly lifted him into his arms, but Ryan turned his head away and politely coughed a time or two.

"Look at that!" the teacher said. "He doesn't want me to see he was struggling."

He had pretty much summed up the introverted personality of my ten-month old baby.

Ryan was quiet, but he was also one, like Kristin, who cared deeply. He formed a few, close relationships with people his age and was fiercely loyal to those he let get to know him underneath his reserved exterior. He was a good baby-sitter to his cousin, Jamie, and later became a wonderful, caring father, loving his kids beyond all else.

When Ryan was a young teen, the city a few miles from us built a new museum, the Minnetrista Cultural Center. Ryan was very interested in building and design and he loved the modern-day mansion look of the museum, as well as the amazing, huge sculpture outside of it. He told me, "I'm going to live there someday." In school, he created house designs of his own and when he was grown, he helped build some houses in our town. I still enjoy passing them, and I remember seeing him at work on them and the pride he took in that work. His very favorite job was restoring old downtown apartments back to their original glory days. Doing that gave him such a sense of accomplishment and it made me happy to see him so happy.

Jeremy was the child who made me laugh. Of course, he did this most often when I had reached the point of exasperation because of some antic of his. He would always try to make me break down and laugh just as I was trying to explain to him why what he had done was not acceptable.

His mind was always working, but his teachers would have said that it was not always working on the right thing. He loved numbers and grasped the basics of math long before kindergarten. In his classes he was always wanting to breeze ahead. One teacher complained that when it came time for a spelling test, he would have all the words written down before she started giving them out. He was bored, but of course, that often leads to goofing off. Jeremy became a master at that.

I was so hurt one day when his fifth-grade teacher, angry at him for running ahead and not paying attention during a field trip, told me she was worried that if he didn't straighten up, he was headed for real trouble one day. In the years to come, oh, how I wanted to let that teacher know exactly how Jeremy had grown up. (She had moved away.) I would have told her how he and his best friend, Tommy, were made co-captains of the high school football team, how he was president of his fraternity in college, and how he even managed to make the Dean's list. And that he went on to be successful in his work and now has a beautiful family of his own.

Jeremy has a little scar on the bridge of his nose, and, being Jeremy, he used to invent a new story of how he got it each time someone inquired about it. I suppose he felt it was a little more glamorous to say it happened in a boating accident than to admit his mother wrapped her little car around a utility pole, right after allowing him to climb into the front seat.

Yes, it wasn't one of my better mothering moments. He was five years old. He and Ryan attended a small Christian school, housed in our church, about five miles away from our home. One icy, winter morning, I had driven Ryan to school, but Jeremy was coming back home with me. He had a doctor's appointment later in the day because of a bad cough and slight fever.

Of course, I was feeling sorry for him, so when he asked in a pitiful little voice if he could come up front with me, I said yes. He had climbed into the front passenger seat and was starting to buckle his seat belt when I hit a patch of ice. I am sorry to say I did the exact wrong thing. I hit the brake, and I spun us into the utility pole. Even with my seat belt on, my head hit and shattered my side of the windshield. I looked and saw the glass on Jeremy's side was shattered also. He raised his head from the dashboard, where he had dropped after hitting the windshield. Blood was dripping from his face.

Someone saw us and called 911. Soon, we were lying in side by side beds at the emergency room. Our main injuries were cuts and the doctor asked which one wanted to be stitched up first. I told him to do mine first, hoping I could show Jeremy that it wasn't too painful. I do remember that watching my little boy's face being stitched hurt me much worse than my own stitches. I sat up on my bed and watched, feeling so guilty. I was so anxious for him, but I remember looking up at the clock, noticing the time, about 9:30 am, and suddenly feeling such peace. The ER doctor also diagnosed Jeremy with pneumonia. That was why he felt bad in the first place. With medicine for his pneumonia and bandages for both of us, we were sent home to recover.

At home, we began to get calls from people at our church. How did they know about our accident? I wondered, but we soon heard the story. Grandpa Bob, the much-loved custodian and piano player at the church, had driven on that same road on his way to the church that morning. He came upon the sight of my little bright green car, obviously just having come into violent contact with the pole. He hurried on to the church and told a group of women who were just gathering for their Bible study meeting. They immediately began to pray. When one of the women told me this, I asked her what time that was. She said it had been just before 9:30, right about the time I had that feeling of peace.

A few days later, we went to look at my car at the wrecking yard where it had been taken. I first saw the twin circles of shattered glass in the windshield. I said one more prayer of thanksgiving that we had not been more seriously injured. Then, I inspected the inside of the car. The back seat, which Jeremy had asked to leave and I had let him do so, was torn up and pushed forward toward the floor. He probably would have been more seriously hurt if he had stayed there. That alleviated my guilt a little, but I still regret I hadn't stopped and gotten him securely in his seat belt.

My left knee sustained a cut from being jammed into something just below the steering wheel, so, ever since, my knee has sported a little white scar that looks exactly like a wishbone. For a long time, Jeremy asked to see, and also wanted to show everyone else, my wishbone. I've never come up with any exotic alternative story for my crash injury.

Chapter 5

Tails of True Love

Besides our three children, we were blessed with various four-legged babies. They certainly gave us lots of love, affection and funny experiences. I believe they were sent to us straight from God as a loving gift, but also because they could help us learn about His ways. I think there should be human training schools, where dogs teach people how to best live in this world, how to be the best human they can be. At least, it seems to me, dogs are a lot better than many people at putting into practice their God-given potential for compassion and love.

Of course, not only dogs; we can't forget cats. I once told our long-haired tuxedo cat, Mittens, that she deserved the Mother of the Year award. She had to have surgery on her stomach soon after having a litter of kittens. We were supposed to keep her separate from the kittens, so they were in a box in our bedroom and Mittens was banned from the room. Of course, we were feeding the kittens the best we could. But we had to listen to Mittens crying outside the door every night. One night, we woke up to what we called the *Mommy's home!* shrieks of joy from the kitties. Mittens had somehow gotten in, and soon we were hearing loud yelps of pain from her as she determinedly let her babies nurse wherever they could find a place around her bandages. She broke in to the room the next night too, so we finally let her have her way; Mittens was just too miserable when she wasn't allowed to take care of her babies.

We had just cats in the early years of our marriage and child-raising, but once we got Jessie, our beautiful collie, we began to see even more examples of devotion and unconditional love. We still had cats, and Jessie saw it as her duty to keep them in line, putting her strong herding instinct to good use. And even though Jessie herself was afraid of storms, she would stand and let a shaking Mittens hide underneath her when the thunder and lightning were scaring them both.

Jessie proved her worth one Thanksgiving morning, although we already knew her worth. Our first grandson was nine months old at the time, and happily crawling around the house. He especially liked going into the kitchen and searching through the recycling box to find some exciting treasures, like flattened plastic bottles or cardboard tubes from paper towel rolls. On that morning, I heard Jessie giving out her *There's trouble* bark and went to investigate. There was baby Jay, crawling toward the accidentally left-open kitchen door that led to a short hallway and then to the old, wooden basement stairs. Jay wasn't quite to the door yet, so I watched for a minute to see how Jessie was handling it. Her barks weren't having much effect on him, so she ran and got her red, rubber squeaky bone. She brought it up to him and plopped it down in front of his little crawling arms. That got his attention and he sat up to look it over for a minute, but of course, soon lost interest and dropped it to resume his journey to the hallway door. Jessie then grabbed the bone, squeaking it as she backed up toward the dining room, trying to lure him away from the open door. Jay turned and crawled toward Jessie, for a foot or so, but then stopped and went toward the dangerous door again. Jessie picked up the bone again, the *squeak, squeak* sounding out along with her pleading bark, as she took the bone closer to the dining room and safety. This time Jay decided to follow Jessie and the bone, Jessie pulling it further and further into the dining room. And finally, she had him out of the kitchen. When I realized what was happening, I had run for my video camera and I managed to record most of this clever rescue by Jessie, who had decided Jay was her charge from the first day.

We wanted Jessie to have one litter of puppies before being spayed, and a friend's male collie seemed a good candidate to help make that happen. Except, Jessie and Eliot were playmate friends, and she wasn't interested in him as a mate. But she got out of the fence one day and soon was expecting puppies by the neighbor's golden retriever. So, we didn't get full-breed collie puppies, but these were adorable, and one of them ended up being our second dog in the household, sweet-hearted Jenny.

Jessie and Jenny seemed to be the type of females born for motherhood, and Jessie's body evidently didn't think medical procedures should get in the way. After she was spayed, she began to have episodes of false pregnancy. This can sometimes happen with her breed. She would act out the whole course of a normal gestation period. She gained weight and even produced milk inside her little dinner plates, as the kids called them. Then we would have to console her and baby her herself when no puppies arrived.

This tendency of hers became quite a predicament when Jenny was found to be expecting. Jessie's hormones kicked in and she went through a whole virtual pregnancy of her own. They seemed to be on a neck and neck schedule, like two pregnant sisters racing to produce the first grandchild. Obviously, Jenny won this race, and Jessie's heart could hardly take it. Here were these beautiful little babies. But what? Jenny seemed to be claiming them as HERS! Jessie was so confused.

Jenny was a good little mother herself. She cleaned and nursed her children and saw to all their needs. If Jessie approached the corner designated for the little family, Jenny would look up calmly, but give out a little warning growl. If Jessie got brave and leaned in to try to sniff a pup, Jenny's warning growl turned into a *Get out!* snarl. These were sad times for Jessie, but one day I think she said to herself, "Hey, I'm the grandma here, and grandmas have rights!" She took her chance when Jenny was out for a brief visit to the back yard. She made her way into the corner and lay down alongside the puppies. They were fascinated with her and immediately snuggled close. Jenny came in and found what appeared to be an uninvited nanny tending her family. Jessie probably indulged in a few little, smug, "How does it feel now?" thoughts. Whatever she was thinking, she didn't feel inclined to give up her position immediately, so, Jenny had to settle for lying down in front of the grandma and pups. When Jessie next needed to go to the back yard, Jenny took over again. But from that day on, those puppies had two mommies. Grandma cuddled and washed, and biological Mom handled the feeding times. They were the very definition of one, big, happy family, and the humans in the house got to enjoy front-row seats to this sweet, ingenious arrangement.

Jessie had a stroke when she was 13-and-a-half. We knew it wasn't going to be a good situation; the vet said she probably wasn't going to make it. All I could think of was that I wanted to take her down to the river at Morrow's Meadow one more time, the place she had enjoyed so much through the years. But, rain was pouring down that day and the following day, too. My friend, Geri, knew how much I wanted one more trip to the river with Jessie, and she prayed with me that the rain would stop so we could go. The next day, the rain stopped. I picked up my beautiful collie and carried her to our van. I noticed how very lightweight she was. It felt like I was carrying a small toddler. Jay went along with me; we didn't take Jenny. We found a nice place to sit in the grass under a large shade tree and Jessie lay across my lap. She couldn't move her head much because of the stroke, but when Jay started tossing rocks out across the river, she lifted her head a bit and her eyes followed the arc of each one he launched. I believe it was a very happy day for Jessie, and a day I am so thankful God gave to us.

Jenny couldn't understand why Jessie didn't come home from her inevitable, final visit to the vet. It was late fall, and I didn't make any more trips to the river that year. When spring came, I took Jenny over for a walk. We parked in the playground parking lot, and when we got out of the car, Jenny began pulling on her leash, wanting to go down the path by the river. She pulled until we got to the exact spot where Jessie and I had been, to the same tree, then she stopped. I don't know how she knew where it was, but I think maybe she had waited all winter to get to the river and stand where her mommy enjoyed that happy, last day.

If Jessie was the beautiful, fierce protector and nurturer, Jenny was the easy-going, compassionate friend. Devotion just shone through her eyes. She loved being a big pillow for tired, cranky grandchildren, who would sometimes fall asleep against her beating heart. When I broke five ribs in a bicycle accident, it was Jenny who did the long night watches with me. I had to sleep in a recliner in the living room for several weeks because I couldn't straighten my back. Jenny was always there, lying on the floor beside my chair, both of us watching the fire in the fireplace, and getting only little cat naps through the night.

When she saw how much it hurt me to try to get out of the chair, and she knew someone usually had to help me, she knew what she needed to do. She came and stood in front of me, her side pushed against my knees, offering her back to me to push against so I could rise out of the chair. She did that for the rest of my recovery period. Just look how God sometimes chooses to meet our needs. Sometimes the rescuers and friends do have four legs.

Our sweet Jenny was wise and tenderhearted, and she knew the value of sacrifice more than a lot of people do. A few years after we lost Jessie, we adopted a cute little puppy we named Hayley. When we brought the puppy home from the animal rescue, Jenny met her with a vigorous, barking welcome. This was quite intimidating to our new little girl. She was afraid of Jenny. Jenny tried all she could to get Hayley to play with her. It looked like she was giving up for the time when we saw her leave the room. She came back with her Winnie the Pooh in her mouth. Winnie the Pooh was a rubber toy bear that had been Jenny's surrogate baby ever since we had found homes for that one litter of puppies she had. Like Jessie, she also went through those false pregnancies after being spayed. When the time came that puppies should have appeared, Jenny took on Winnie as her baby. She cuddled and washed it, and she was frantic and would cry if it happened to be on the opposite side of a door from her.

So, our hearts just overflowed with emotion when we saw Jenny gently set Winnie the Pooh down in front of the new puppy. The Bible tells us that obedience is better than sacrifice, but Jenny was one creature who knew how to give it all.

Chapter 6

Dark Clouds

Even surrounded by all this love of family and dogs and cats, I began to experience some depression. "But what do you have to be depressed about?" I don't know if I actually got this question from other people, or if I just projected it onto them when I told them anything about how I was feeling. But then, I asked *myself* this question, also. *I should be ashamed. Look at all I have, a good husband who works hard for all of us, three children I would give my life for, and this string of beloved pets parading down through the years with us in our comfortable home.* So, of course, guilt compounded the depression I was trying to deny.

It didn't go away, though. Those feelings of living in a gray world returned. I wanted to enjoy all that we had, but something was stopping me. Since I had always tried to be "good", why did I so often feel that I didn't deserve to enjoy things? It really didn't make sense. It made me think back to one day at an amusement park when I was a child. I was only about five. My mother wanted me to go on a certain ride. I was saying no, and she was exasperated with me. She chided me for being a big baby, because she thought I wouldn't go on it because I was afraid.

I remember so clearly standing there, thinking, *Doesn't she know? Doesn't she know that this big, colorful, exciting thing is not for me?* Why did five-year-old me, who yearned for color, think she didn't deserve to experience it? And why, in adulthood, when I had achieved some good things that should have made me a little proud, did I fall into such negative thinking again?

I didn't know how to push through the barrier that was keeping me from appropriating simple pleasures for myself. Any sort of contentment or happiness seemed physically out of my reach. One day, I told my mother-in-law I felt like everyone in the room was way, far away from me, and I was shrinking back, looking at life going on but not living it. And that wasn't just a mental picture of myself. I was so deep into depression, in the dark places in my mind, that even my body perception was askew.

It honestly felt that I would have to reach out across a vast distance to touch a person who was just a few feet from me. Fortunately, my mother-in-law didn't have me committed on the spot. She told me she understood, and that she had been through similar feelings. She told me mixed up emotions and anxiety can truly cause such physical misconceptions. I don't know; she had definitely experienced a lot of anxiety in her life. So, whether her explanation of my strange feelings was accurate or not, I was grateful she told me she understood. She was one of my biggest champions.

Of course, depression once again began to show itself as illness. My confusion was compounded though, because so many things actually *were* going on with me physically. It wasn't until several years later that I learned some things that helped explain why I had those mysterious physical symptoms. But at the time I was going through this, I only felt foolish and misunderstood. I was sick and I felt I would never be all right. I seemed to live day to day with fear. Why couldn't I believe that God would take care of me? I don't know why I battled over this in my mind so much, since I had been raised to know a loving God. Somehow, I just felt left out.

I think I was still feeling I had to earn His love and blessings, and mostly all I could think of was how I fell short all of the time. Then, in my mind, my very worries were proof that I didn't even trust Him. It was a never-ending circle in my thoughts. *I've messed up again. If I had enough faith, I wouldn't be sick and depressed. I'm sick and depressed, so I must not have enough faith, so I'll never get out of this.*

One doctor took my husband aside one day and suggested that rather than having real physical issues, I was suffering from a depressive illness. They didn't think about my being just on the other side of the door and that I could hear them. At first, I had a rush of frustrated tears spill down my face. Another doctor was discounting my pain. Then, I got angry. I wanted to go out and ask that doctor if he thought he might be a little depressed if he felt sick and weak and everybody was telling him there was nothing wrong with him. Then, I considered that his words might have some truth in them, that maybe I was still denying the seriousness of my depression. Well then, what could I do?

What can help me? Will drugs help me? They tried many drugs. Most of them just made me feel worse, more distant from reality than I already was. I became more confused and more depressed. I felt I was all alone in trying to figure this out. It seemed to me that everyone was just saying, "Get better", but I didn't know how to get better. When I tried to figure it out, my thoughts would just scatter in all directions, and I could only imagine bad outcomes.

Would prayer break through this war going on in my mind? Would scripture help? I had many dear, praying friends, to whom I will forever be indebted, and I constantly read my Bible through those confusing times. I held on to scriptures, truly believing them. But it always came back around to this: *Why am I not getting healed? How will I ever get out of this?* I don't even know how I did break through all of this. It had to be God's grace that stuck with me even when all I could do was doubt that He cared.

Besides my mental distress, I had to deal with the real physical issues of those years. After a serious bout of pneumonia one year, I had chronic asthma attacks the following three winters, as well as repeated cases of bronchitis. I also discovered I had a thyroid disorder, which explained at least some of the depression and my nearly non-existent energy. It's not surprising that all of these things came together to throw me into so much confusion that I didn't know where to turn.

The craziness of severe depression and out of control anxiety finally did let up, but I will always regret those days. If I could, I would take back those many times that my children saw me go from one dramatic ER visit or hospitalization to another.

I was grateful for the break in those dark clouds and things went rolling along for a few smooth years. But then, frustration returned once again with the worsening of my hereditary condition, HAE.

Chapter 7

HAE

It seems the HAE was almost dormant for several years after my pregnancies, but it did come back in full force, and it was beginning to take over my whole life. This condition was still a mystery to almost all doctors. I loved my HAE doctor, an immunologist, and she did understand HAE, but when I had to deal with doctors who did not know me, it was a different story. Once again I was going to the ER with, for example, internal swelling that was giving me chest pains and exerting pressure on my lungs. I would be told again they couldn't see anything wrong with me. And, doctors just didn't know in those days that cranial swelling could cause the migraine-like headaches I was having. Hearing, "We just don't know what is wrong with you" only made me more discouraged and ashamed of myself for even seeking help.

Then, in the late 1990s, I began to communicate with other HAE patients around the country. When some of us first met in person, it was a revelation to us all that others had been through the same thing each of us had experienced. There were often tears of understanding and relief when one person after another, in some of our larger meetings, would say, "They thought I was crazy. They thought I was faking. They thought I was drug seeking."

It seemed many HAE patients had been living parallel lives. All the time that most of us had been suffering, we didn't even think about there being other people with HAE, living like we did. Most of us had never met anyone else with the disorder, aside from our own relatives. Meeting and sharing with other patients made a huge difference in our outlook, even though things were still very difficult since there was so little effective treatment for our attacks.

My husband was the one who had held the family together when I was going through so much depression, and now, once again, he had to do the same during the worsening HAE attacks. He took care of the house and the children, but he also wanted so badly to help me. I imagine, though, that he felt the same way I used to feel watching my mother and sister: confused and helpless. But maybe he doesn't know how much he really did help me. It had to have been difficult for him. More than once during attacks, he had to gather me up off the floor after I had fainted. This would happen if I became severely dehydrated and developed hypovolemia, dangerously low blood pressure.

We learned it helped to rub my hands and wrists with an icy cold washcloth whenever I was heading toward another blackout. These are the times, of course, that I should have been going to the hospital for IV fluid replacement, but both of us were so sick of the idea of going to the hospital. My husband did all this, laundry, cooking, taking care of me and the kids, in addition to working his full-time job. And one more thing: he had to live with a wife on anabolic steroids.

It had been known for a long time that anabolic steroids had the ability to produce C1-inhibitor in the human body. So, back in those days, the doctors who at least knew about Hereditary Angioedema–and they were few–prescribed these "body-building" male hormone drugs to their HAE patients, men and women alike. The reasoning was that getting the patient's C1-inhibitor replaced would prevent attacks.

Well, I had a sensitivity to just about any drug. Allergy medicine put me in a fog for days. The steroids used for such things as treating asthma gave me nightmares and fits of crying. My doctor knew the only thing that would help me was taking these male hormones, but it was not a pleasant experience for me. Athletes who overuse these steroids talk of experiencing "roid rage", unreasonable bouts of anger. Roid rage is real. For me, if it wasn't outright anger, the "rage" would come out in displays of zero patience, and in words just being spouted off with no forethought, no filter.

One night at a Mexican restaurant, I requested guacamole for my chimichanga. The waiter informed me it would be seventy-five cents extra. I wasn't having any of that! I'm ashamed to say, I retorted (and probably not in a quiet voice) with, "What do you mean it's seventy-five cents extra?" My poor husband was slinking down in his seat, reaching for my arm, trying to placate me.

"I'll PAY the seventy-five cents!" he covertly hissed in my direction.

Some time later I tried to convince my doctor I needed to stop the steroids. I was working as a substitute teacher, and although I did a fairly good job of controlling my moods, there were times I was afraid I might one day throw a blackboard eraser at a third grader if he or she tried my patience one more time. I did not want to make the evening news.

I did stop the steroids eventually, but years later, before we had our present-day treatments, I had to be on them again for a while. This time my husband got called out on what he really thought of my short fuse. He, our grandson, Jay, who was about eight at the time, and I had gone to a large chain grocery store. They finished first, so they went back to the car before I did. When I was done with my shopping, I went out the door and could not find where our car was parked. It turned out I had gone out the wrong door, but all I knew was I couldn't find our car and I was frustrated.

I called my husband's cell phone, and most likely argued with him that I couldn't have come out the wrong door. It had to be somebody else's fault. I was crying by the time I said, "All right! I see you now. I'm coming."

When I got to the car, Jay said to me, "Grandma, what does 'irrational' mean?"

My husband slunk down and whispered, "Jay, I didn't really mean for you to ask Grandma!"

As my HAE seemed to be letting up once again, my two oldest, Kristin and Ryan, began having attacks. They had been tested at a young age and were shown to have the deficiency, but I had held on to the hope it would not affect them badly. Jeremy's test was negative for HAE, for which, of course, I was very grateful.

One of Kristin's early swelling attacks came when she was 16, while my husband and I were more than 100 miles away. We had gone with Jeremy to his fifth-grade camping trip in southern Indiana. We were about to set out for home when I called Kristin to check on how things were going.

She and Ryan were staying alone for the weekend. She told me she felt her throat was swelling a little and she wasn't sure what to do. I told her if she needed to go to the hospital, she should ask our neighbor to take her. She said it really wasn't too bad, but still, it was a frightening trip home for us. I called again a couple of times, and I remember telling 12-year old Ryan to please watch her closely, which I am sure put a lot of pressure on him, the one who took things so seriously already.

Kristin told me he kept following her around, repeatedly making her take more drinks of water to make sure her throat wasn't closing up. She was all right when we got home, but that turned out to be just the first of many scares with her.

Her swelling episodes became worse and more frequent during her college years, probably from the pressure and stress common at that time of life. In her sophomore year she had an apartment just off campus. One day she called to tell me she had gone to the doctor because her lip had swollen. He had given her an injection, probably some combination of steroids, which really wasn't very effective, but was the best thing our doctor had for acute attacks. I told her I would come over and stay with her for a while.

When I saw that the swelling had not gone down much, I wanted her to come home and spend the night so I could keep an eye on her. She didn't think it was necessary, but I said if she wouldn't come home with me, I was going to stay at her apartment for the night. That was fine with her, and she went into the bedroom and slept for a while. About an hour later, she came out, pointing to her face, indicating she was unable to talk. The swelling had increased so much and her tongue had grown so large that she could not close her mouth. I grabbed her and drove her to the university hospital ER department, just three blocks from her apartment.

By the time we got there, her face was turning blue. They were able to help her in time, and I could only thank God that we had stayed in town. We would have been seven miles away from the hospital if I had taken her home with me.

Ryan's 18th birthday fell on a Thanksgiving Day. He didn't want to come down to dinner. When I pressed him to tell me why, he showed me his left hand, swollen tight, with evidence of more swelling starting to move up his arm. Once again, I felt heartbroken. Another of my children was going to have to deal with this disease. It didn't show up often in the winter of that school year, his senior year, but in the springtime, track season was a different story.

Tall and lean, Ryan had been a runner since early childhood. This year he was running relays, doing the long jump and the high hurdles. Too many times swelling would occur, his body would feel off-balance, and he would hit the barrier during the high hurdles. I think he worried that his reputation as a track standout was in jeopardy, although he still did very well for the season. He loved his coach, Mr. Owen, and wanted so badly to win for him.

One night, Ryan had a severe abdominal attack. It was around midnight as I sat with him on the bathroom floor. He was in so much pain and he had almost reached the point of dehydration. Between bouts of pain and nausea, he talked to me about track. After a while, I couldn't quite understand his words, and there was a rising urgency in his voice. It was when he tried to leave the bathroom, and go to his room to get dressed and go to the school, that I realized why he was so distressed. It was midnight, but in the anxiety and disorientation brought on by this extreme attack, he believed there was a track meet and he didn't want to let Mr. Owen and his team down.

I hated that my children had to endure these terrible attacks.

Chapter 8

Adventures in Road Tripping

All this drama with illness, depression, ER visits and close calls makes it sound like we were in a state of misery most of the time. But no, there were many happy times, too. The kids' friends chose our house as a hang-out spot. The boys had a clubhouse in the upstairs section of our garage. To this day, our garage bears the marks of some of their adolescent remodeling efforts. Kristin's friends talked and giggled and played loud music in her small bedroom that was papered with rainbows and clouds. As a family, we played board games, worked jigsaw puzzles, had birthday parties, and took road trips.

The family Chevy Citation became a little cramped for our summer vacation trips. So, we bought a GMC Chevy truck camper. We christened her Old Orangey because of her bright orange cab and because we hoped she would last as long as our cat of the same name, who was 14 years and holding.

Then we set out to see America. Well, sort of. Sometimes we had to use a little persuasion to get Dad to stop at points of real interest. After a 1300 mile trek in which we visited southern Ontario and

Quebec, we moved on to New England. It was my husband's idea of historical sight-seeing to do a quick drive-through of Boston. He quickly became rattled by the city's many circular traffic patterns at intersections. He still shakes when he hears that awful word, "rotary." But, there we were, hurtling through Boston in Old Orangey.

"I think I see the Old North Church!" I shouted as we whizzed past the Historical District.

"Daddy, that was Fenway Park!" Jeremy yelled through the rear-to-cab intercom.

I thought I saw a tiny Red Sox player step up to the plate as I grabbed a glance through the rear-view mirror. Boston itself was a blur, but we knew he wouldn't want to miss Plymouth Rock, a little way outside of town. We were wrong. I think I saw tears in Kristin's eyes as her daddy drove past the exit leading to the shores where our forefathers had landed.

Kristin and I had secretly hoped to spend the night on romantic Cape Cod. Well, we didn't tell Dad that. We just worked it so that I, the navigator, gently lulled him south on Route 3. Kristin and I exchanged smiles at the "Cape Cod" signs we saw along the way.

At about the fourth such sign, my husband seemingly came awake from his driving reverie and said, "Oh no, I didn't want to go to Cape Cod!"

But it was too late. We were already on the Sagamore Bridge. We spent two nights on romantic Cape Cod. Even my husband enjoyed it, if you don't count the time we ran out of gas because one of the boys had accidentally tripped the switch from the full gas tank to the empty one.

Old Orangey went on to take us to such memorable places as Niagara Falls, Mackinac Bridge in Michigan, the Gateway Arch in St. Louis and Smoky Mountain National Park. I have to say, she did outlive the cat, who passed away a month short of her 21st birthday.

God's protective angels have always been busy taking care of the Noble family, but maybe never more so than when we were on the road. One night they even seemed to direct us to the right place to have a flat tire.

We had enjoyed a vacation at a North Carolina beach, and were heading toward home. On this trip we were traveling in our van. It was almost midnight, and all three kids were asleep in the back, when we started to round a curve on Jellico Mountain, near the Tennessee-Kentucky border. I had the strong impression something was about to happen, and I knew I needed to pray.

I put my hand on my husband's shoulder—he was driving—and prayed for our protection. Just then we heard, *Shwooop,* the sound of a tire blowing out. We were able to get off the road, to a tiny piece of shoulder that was right up against a wall of solid rock. Strangely enough, we had already bought two new tires on this trip, but did not have a spare, and of course we didn't have a cell phone back then.

So, there we were, between the pavement and a rock wall, just beyond a curve, where drivers coming up on us would not see us until the last moment. Even though we weren't stopped on the actual road, my mother's heart was terrified at the thought of my children, sleeping in the back of the van, just a little off the road, on a curve where every driver coming would not see us until they were almost upon us. I prayed all night.

All three kids eventually woke up and we spent the night watching cars and trucks fly by without stopping. We couldn't count all the semis bearing the name of a popular snack company that whooshed by. We thought surely those drivers would be nice people and help us. When none of them did, we joked, "We're never eating those snacks again."

As dawn was lighting the skies, a southbound semi driver blew his horn at us, indicating that he would call for help. Soon a state trooper pulled up behind us. He called for a tow truck and in a little while we were being towed off the mountain.

I had not liked that place where we had spent the night, right off the road and against that scary tall wall. But as the tow truck driver pulled us away, I looked to the right. Just a few yards past our spot, daylight revealed a different view. We had spent the night just short of a large break in the rocky wall of the mountain. What that opening revealed was a panorama of the sprawling valley far below. God had let us stop just before we came to a dangerous drop-off to oblivion.

Chapter 9

Heavenly Visitors

God's grace sometimes comes knocking right at our door. Or, as in the case of one wet September evening, knocking at my car window. Rain lashed my car that day for four straight hours, ever since I left Kristin's house, where I had been visiting for a few days.

Home was still three hours away, as the bridge across the Ohio River was coming up. The bridge was at a small town. I couldn't resist getting out on the Kentucky side to have a look at the big, steel structure, its lights winking in the rainy evening. After taking a few pictures, I returned to my car and drove across the bridge.

I should have stayed on the highway, heading steadily toward home, but in my curiosity, I wanted to see a little more of the riverfront, so I made a turn off the main street. Very quickly, I realized I had indeed gotten to the riverfront. There was an iron barricade at the end of the street and warnings not to go any further, so I attempted a tight little U-turn on the dark, dead-end lane. I thought I was doing fine, until my car skidded off into a narrow, muddy ditch. Trying to reverse out of the ditch only mired my car more. By then I was nearly in tears. For one thing, I did not want to call my husband

and tell him I was stuck in a ditch beside the Ohio River!

I was commiserating (well, whining) with Kristin via my cell phone when I felt a presence outside my car window. I looked out to see a very large man in a tan khaki coat, with a strange blue light shining out from above his dark face. I think maybe my head hit the roof of the car. Blue-light man apologized for startling me and all I could say was an ungrateful, "Where did you come from?"

He indicated a barn about 25 yards away. He said his name was Thomas. I finally realized the blue light was a small version of a coal miner's lamp, a little flashlight strapped around his head. So, he wasn't a heavenly being, but it appeared Thomas was to be my rescuer that night.

Then the comedy began. Comedy of errors, that is. Thomas checked my car to see where he could fasten a tow rope. Nothing was immediately apparent, so he said he would need to get something to lie on to get underneath the car for a look. To the barn he went, and I expected him to bring out a large piece of cardboard or maybe a tarp.

Then here he came, dragging two long, folding tables, the kind you see at church dinners. These were placed on the wet ground, and he lay down on one, with his big khaki-covered body disappearing under my car. His triumphant smile was so sweet when he slid back out after succeeding in getting the tow rope attached.

I had been thinking I should call my roadside assistance club, but he told me, no, he could take care of this. While he was working on his strategy, trying to decide if his Jeep could do the job, a local police officer came along. There followed a big discussion between the officer, Thomas, and a neighbor who had moseyed out of his house down the street to cheer Thomas on.

While the three of them were being pelted by rain, still trying to make a plan, I stayed inside my car. The policeman advised me to contact my auto club, so I called them. I was put on hold for 25 minutes, with the agent checking back with me once in a while, arguing there was no such town in the state I had given her as my location.

I'm sure the good men outside were miserable in the cold, drizzling rain, but even though I was dry and warm inside my car, I just wanted to break down and cry. When the auto club person did locate a towing service, she gave me the news that the tow truck would arrive in one and a half to two hours.

Back to Thomas. He had finally hooked up his Jeep to my car, and I saw he was ready to rev up his car and yank me out of the ditch. Well, he revved, but the rope broke, and his car heaved forward to the opposite side of the road, into a matching muddy ditch that just seemed to be waiting for him.

"Uh, Claudia," he said, "my car is stuck now."

I didn't know whether to laugh or cry, but I just couldn't be upset with this dejected, innocent knight in a khaki coat.

Thomas, his neighbor, and I spent a total of three hours on that wet dead-end road by the river. The tow truck finally came and pulled me out and, after getting my signature, the driver told me to go on my way.

Of course, I couldn't leave Thomas like that. I stayed in my now free car and watched as they hooked up to Thomas' Jeep and pulled it out. I went to tell him I'd give him money to pay at least part of his towing bill, but he said the man had not charged him, since he had been trying to help me. I still tried to give him $15 for his trouble, but he wouldn't take it.

"I'll see you again, Claudia," he said.

I don't know about that, but I will always have a soft spot in my heart for the big man from the barn beside the Ohio River.

Thomas might not have been a heavenly visitor, but sometimes I still wonder about Joanne, my seatmate years ago on a tiny plane heading to Springfield, MO. This was a sad trip for me. My 18-year old nephew, Adam, had been killed in an auto accident and I was on my way west to be with my sister.

It happened that our little plane came upon a ferocious thunderstorm and we were being knocked to and fro. Joanne, a beautiful African-American woman wearing a business suit, noticed I had my face buried in my hands. She assumed I was afraid.

She tugged on my arm and said, "Don't be afraid. God's got us."

I looked at her kind face and decided to tell her the whole story and that I wasn't afraid, just upset. I also told her I was worried because I didn't know how I was going to get from the Springfield airport to the downtown bus station, where I needed to board a bus to continue to my sister's house.

Joanne answered, "Well, I know how. You're going to ride with me as soon as I get the rental car waiting for me."

We picked up her car, and as we drove away from the airport, she told me, "You know, whenever I fly, I ask the Lord to put me beside someone who needs a friend, and it never fails; He always does."

When we arrived at the bus station I saw my bus, already loaded and with its motor running. "Oh no, it's going to leave!" I said.

"Honey," she announced, "this bus doesn't leave 'til I say it leaves," and she swerved into the parking lot and stopped directly in front of the bus, blocking its departure. Then she said she wanted to pray with me. I saw the driver and some of his passengers lean forward to watch as we bowed to pray. I boarded the bus with renewed strength to face the days ahead.

Joanne had given me her business card and sometime later I wrote to her, but I never received a reply. Kind of makes me wonder if she and Thomas are friends.

Maybe we do have heavenly visitations. After a rough night of fighting strep throat when he was about nine, Ryan told me he had seen an angel standing beside his bed during the night. And Jeremy casually told me one morning that Jesus had come to his room the night before. He showed me exactly where, and it was a place between his bed and the wall, where no person really could have stood. He told me Jesus was wearing something like a white gown and there was "a blue thing, like this." Jeremy swept his hand diagonally across his chest. He then asked me why I thought Jesus had come to see him. I could only say that He must have wanted to visit him to say hello.

Another time when Ryan claimed to see an angel he was about seven or eight. Both boys were in the car with me. I started across a highway that was not very busy, but then my car sunk into a huge pothole. There was a car coming toward us by that time.

I was frightened, of course, and I'm sure I sent up a very quick prayer, to please get us out of there. Then, it seemed we were instantly on the other side, safe.

Ryan excitedly said, "Did you see that angel pick our car up and put us down right here?"

I believe ministering angels are everywhere. It might be that children catch sight of them more often than we adults do.

Chapter 10

Beauty Where We Find It

God was showing me His loving care, whether it was through angelic visitors or through other people. Then, as I got older, I began to see His touch in everyday life. I think He wanted me to open my eyes to see the blessings right at hand.

"You must live in a beautiful place," a far-away email friend wrote to me, after seeing photos I had posted online.

Um, really? My little town, a beautiful place? I would like to say my town is one of those quaint villages with a public square, a burbling fountain and maybe a monument big enough to drive circles around. Flowers tumbling over their painted boxes at every home's windows, pretty, meandering streets, and on, and on.

Well, not quite. We do have at least one soaring church steeple, a few impressive homes on hilltops, and a nice-looking walking bridge that leads to Morrow's Meadow, the grassy park set between a river and a creek. This town had been my home for many years, and I think that after a while, the beauty had become easy to miss. After my email friend's comment, I decided to go out for a walk, with my camera in my hand.

Wow. The tall sunflowers at the elementary school were just begging me to come close and snap their picture. Further up the street, I began to see many different kinds and colors of flowers. When I saw one of my favorites, a deep pink coneflower, with a bumblebee hovering over it, I didn't even worry about getting stung. I lowered my face to the flower and watched as the little bee industriously traversed the amber-hued, seed-covered center. A patch of velvety lavender and black pansies gave me one of those *"Oh!"* moments. Every single one had the same dark markings inside. Not one of them missed out.

A reminder for me right there: if God cared about those flowers enough to paint them that way, He must care about the trials of me and my family. This walk was becoming a revelation.

As I continued my walk, I saw dogs out for their own stroll, on the end of long leashes held by their masters. These dogs didn't care about any town monument or fountains. They were just happy to be out on a beautiful, warm evening. They were thrilled for the chance to exercise their legs and use their favorite sense—SMELL—to discover the extraordinary new worlds this ordinary town had in store for those who would just take the time to look (or sniff) around.

On subsequent walks through town, I adopted the attitude of anticipation that those dogs had, and looked around for what might be offered. For my effort, I was rewarded with gorgeous sunset colors that winked through the trees along the river, cute little kids hanging upside down on the monkey bars, and once, several squirrels playing a game of tag. My plain little town was very picturesque, after all.

One late afternoon, I decided to go a bit further afield and see what I could find to appreciate. I was driving this time. About twenty miles from home, I found a line of autumn-dressed trees, proudly displaying their beautiful mirror image in a river. I captured, with my camera, the golden evening sun as it sank lazily into a lake. I saw some chestnut-colored horses that were enjoying a playful run before retiring to their stalls for the night.

Even though bouts of depression and times of sadness still plagued me occasionally, these beauty-scouting forays and their rewards made me feel that maybe God was giving me a glimpse of a time when I might again live every day in my lost world of color.

Chapter 11

When You Pray

God gives us so many gifts, and He wants us to take delight in them, such as the very place He has given us to live. You might be surprised to know scripture talks about our homes and the things in them. Did you know the Bible even talks about our closets? Matthew 6:6 (King James Version) says, *"But when you pray, go into your closet, and when you have shut your door, pray to your Father which is in secret; and your Father, which sees in secret, shall reward you openly."*

First, I have to admit: I have a love-hate relationship with my closet. I dream of having the gorgeous, spacious, walk-in closet/dressing rooms they show in those homes magazines or on reality house-flipping shows. But my reality is this. My closet is a sweet little slant-ceiling alcove/nook/hole-in-the-wall. I was excited when our youngest moved out and I took over this little closet that was in the boys' bedroom. It was all mine. I left the slightly bigger closet in our bedroom to my husband, all that space to use for his clothes. Well, also some suitcases, the ironing board (after all, how often would I need to get that out?), extra blankets, bowling balls, et cetera.

My little closet has given me an adventure in organizing. I was proud of the interlocking shelves I purchased from the building supply store and placed against the back wall. For some reason, the former owners of our house installed a hook or a row of hooks almost every place they set their eyes on. These old wire hooks worked out great for hanging my purses, canvas bags, belts and the occasional bag of tennis shoes. There's a nice, sturdy rod for hanging clothes, and Ryan installed an overhead light for me. So, I was all set. My own closet, complete with a sticker on the door, left over from the '80s or so, saying, "Rejoice in the Lord!"

I did say "love-hate" relationship so I will have to include a few of the negatives points of my closet. Those would be that darling slanted ceiling, which means I can't stand upright in one end of the closet, the teensy amount of usable floor space. And those interlocking shelves that were so practical now only serve to hold several sizes of jeans I am trying to get down into again. That can be a little depressing.

There came a day when my little closet turned on me. Now, I understand that Matthew 6:6 refers to praying privately rather than standing on a street corner and shouting out our prayers, but that day I decided to take the verse literally. With no one else in the house on that warm, summer day, I stepped into my tiny closet, shut the door, and began to pray. I started by giving thanks for this special little place where I could be totally alone, not even the dog or the cat bothering me.

Soon I was interceding for many friends and family members.

Eventually, I did notice the air was getting a little close in my closet. I reached for the doorknob to open the door a bit, to give myself a little air.

Jiggle, jiggle. Nothing.

I began to get a bit nervous and tried to push the door while still uselessly twisting the knob. Then there was a *thump.* I found myself standing there with the inside doorknob resting in my hand, obviously no longer connected to the outside doorknob. The thump I heard must have been that outside doorknob falling out into the middle of the bedroom floor.

Um, okay, it will be all right. Don't get upset.

I pushed heavily against the door. I stuck my fingers through the hole where the knob used to be. I put the knob back in and again tried to release the lock. Nothing worked.

Okay, obviously "somebody" doesn't want me to pray, but I'm going to keep praying until I'm done anyway.

So I lifted up some prayers of thanksgiving and a few more petitions for...

Um, it is getting a little too warm in here.

Because of the thick carpet on the closet floor, there was almost no air coming in at the bottom of the door, and now my breathing began to feel a little restricted. I pounded. I yelled.

Don't panic!

I knew my daughter-in-law was at home, just half a block away. So, I yelled at the top of my voice to her and my young grandson, "Laura, Laura! I'm stuck! Come help me! Laura! Thomas!"

No answer from down the street. Well, now it was up to brute strength. None of the previous ramming attempts had worked, but I guess the survival instinct was pretty strong, because with a final push I burst through the door and took huge gulps of wonderful, fresh air.

Since then, I've wondered if that was one of the times when God had to shake His head over me .

I didn't always pray in tiny, hot closets.

"For where two or three are gathered together in My name, there am I in the midst of them." Matthew 18:20 (KJV) This became more than just a Bible verse when my prayer partners and I gathered together. We knew the verse was true in theory, but once we began to diligently seek the Lord in our prayers, we knew it was true in reality. We had started out as a small group that prayed for our children's schools. We did not meet on school grounds, but one year, a week before the school semester started, we walked around the grounds of the local high school seven times, silently lifting up our petitions.

We prayed that there would be a loving atmosphere that encouraged learning, that there would be healthy relationships between the students and between students and teachers, and, of course, we asked for safety for all who would occupy the building in the coming year. Throughout the school year, we saw many things and heard many reports that let us know our requests had been heard.

Some of the praying moms' children graduated and went on to college. Some in our group changed work schedules or jobs, and some moved away. So, in later years, it was just three of us, Dawn and Geri and myself, praying together on those Monday nights. We found that did not mean God's grace had decreased. We had such a bond with each other, and still do, even though we aren't able to meet like we did before.

We learned there are times when sharing your burdens among just those two or three (and the Lord Himself) can mean more than having a thousand people lift you up in prayer. We saw great, almost miraculous, changes in some of our family members' lives. Our faith increased so much when we saw what God could do when we started taking Him at His Word.

Chapter 12

October, 2008

Fall was always my favorite time of year. I loved the bright blue skies, the falling leaves and the crisp feeling in the air. On a gorgeous, glorious Saturday afternoon in October, 2008, my family went over to the high school track, just to enjoy the day. Ryan often took his kids there, or to nearby Morrow's Meadow, to play. On this day Ryan and his children got on their bikes, ready to go. My husband decided he would go, too, and he hopped on his own bike. Our dog Hayley was just a puppy then, so I grabbed her and her leash and drove over in my car.

The puppy's exuberant mood seemed to be matched by all of us. Hayley excitedly ran in the grass alongside the track and inside the track the three generations played a little football.

As I ambled around the track and watched the happy proceedings, I was aware of how blessed we were to be in that place together on such a beautiful day. Of course, I had my camera with me, and I was lucky enough to get a shot just after Ryan had kicked the ball high in the air. He and his 11-year-old son Thomas had their faces raised towards the spinning ball, which showed up in the picture also. I knew I had gotten the perfect shot for the perfect day.

The next evening, Ryan came over to our house to watch the Patriots game on television. He was quiet, even quieter than normal. I felt worried about him. I knew he had some concerns on his mind. Always the mother, I watched for signs of physical distress, especially any swelling. I was anxious to hear him talk to make sure there was no rasp in his voice that would hint at a laryngeal swell. He seemed all right though, and he even fixed a little angel light of mine that I had not been able to connect correctly.

At about midnight, I decided to go to bed. Since Ryan was still in the living room, sitting on the couch to watch the news for a while, I tossed him a blanket from where I stood on the stairway, and told him he might as well sleep there since he had to get up to go to work in just five or six hours.

He pushed the blanket aside and said, "No, I'm okay."

The phone awakened me at 5:00 in the morning. I could barely hear the voice that was speaking; I couldn't recognize the voice, or quite make out what the words were. Then, when I looked at the caller ID, I saw the call was from Ryan's cell phone, and I realized Ryan was saying, "Help me!"

My husband and I started to run to his house, just across the street and five houses down. When we tried to open our front door, there was something in the way. When we pushed it open, we saw Ryan was lying on our porch, his phone dropped beside him. He had no heartbeat. In the next minutes, I knew that for the rest of my life, I would regret not questioning him about how he was feeling just hours before. And I knew my husband would never be able to erase the memory of trying to perform life-saving CPR, when, because of severe swelling, there simply was no room in his son's airway.

The bedroom phone was still in my hand, and I called 911. The EMT station was only a few blocks away, but it seemed to me they must be traveling from miles away. Of course, it was only a few minutes.

The paramedics took over the CPR attempts. They might have intubated him then but I don't know. They did get a heartbeat and they took him to the local hospital, seven miles away. Ryan's heart had been stopped for twenty minutes. I followed him into the emergency room. I touched him and talked to him. I felt he was moving his head towards me and following me with his eyes, but the doctors told me that his motions were just seizures, that he really wasn't seeing me.

Throughout the day, many friends gathered to pray and cry and pray again. We called Kristin, who was living in Georgia, and she got on the road immediately. By late afternoon, she passed through Indianapolis just in time to pick up Jeremy, who had flown in from New Hampshire.

As the day continued, after each examination, the doctors would tell us there was a little less brain activity. When nurses told me it was only the machines keeping Ryan alive, I truly wanted to physically attack them. My arms reached up, wanting to shake them by their shoulders until they took back their words. I'm sure it's the type of reaction nurses, especially in ICU, often see.

What happened to our faith? What happened to God's promises? We were believers. How could this be happening? We were supposed to be able to speak to mountains and they would fall into the sea. Why weren't our prayers being answered?

In the evening, I felt I was at the end of my faith. I went to the hospital chapel and lay down on the floor in front of the cross. Never had I felt so small, helpless, powerless.

"Okay, God," I said, "I can't make Ryan all right. Please, be with him and take care of him. You can heal him, or You can take him. I can't pray for anything else. Except, if he does wake up, please let him be whole again. If he can live, please heal the damage in his brain."

I left the chapel feeling like a failure as a mother. I did not know how to save my child. At the same time, I knew that I had done the only thing I could do for him at that point; I had put him in God's hands. The discouraging reports continued through the night. In the morning the doctor called a family meeting. I will never forget that small room with my husband and myself, Kristin, Jeremy and Jay, Ryan's son who was now 13, around the table.

What we were experiencing was the very definition of heartbreak.

The doctor explained that the medicine they were giving Ryan to keep his heart beating was destroying his kidney function, and his organs were beginning to shut down. If things didn't somehow reverse, the life supporting machines would have to be taken off. My husband and I signed permission for that to happen if he didn't get better. I still held onto the fact that God could heal him with or without machines, so what was the difference, really? There were more episodes during that day. Ryan's temperature rose to 109 degrees. I reminded God of my plea to heal him of any brain damage if he lived.

We had to take him off life support at 9 o'clock that night. My husband, Kristin, Jay and I stood around his bed. Jeremy, who was Ryan's younger brother by only 16 months, sat in a nearby chair and cried. My heart broke for my whole family. The nurse disconnected all machines and monitors and left us alone.

Jay told us he wanted to tell us what he had talked about to Ryan during his visits the past two days. He said he had told Ryan he was his hero, that he had been looking forward to his dad guiding him through his teen years, that he wanted to grow to be a man just like him. Jay placed his hand over Ryan's heart. The beat was already slowing down. Jay said he wanted to feel it until it stopped. He even lifted his hand once to ask me if it was still there. I told him I felt a very faint beat. He put his hand back on his dad's chest and left it there until the end.

That night, after escaping to bed, I felt I could finally do what I had been wanting to do, scream with grief. Putting my face deep into my pillow, I cried and yelled until my throat hurt. Still I wanted to scream louder. I did, until I realized what was happening; the intense strain on my throat was beginning to make it swell. I knew I could not let this happen, could not go to the ER and possibly be in the hospital when we had to have a funeral. I had to push my cries back down inside.

I hated Hereditary Angioedema with all that was within me that night.

The next day began the unimaginable process of preparing to bury our son. We had already purchased, "on paper", burial plots for ourselves, and since Ryan was divorced, we knew his should be beside ours. I certainly cannot say I was happy about it, but it was a comfort that we were able to choose a place on a gently rising hillside, out of view of the road. Looking out from that spot we could see a stand of trees that lined the bank of the river that was running just below. The autumn colors of the leaves were beautiful.

After an evening of just being together as a family, talking and going through old photographs, I finally went to bed and was able to sleep a little. In the morning, just before it was time to wake up and dress for the funeral, I had a dream that seemed absolutely physical in nature. I was standing at the riverbank near where Ryan was to be buried. I looked around at the trees in their blazing October glory.

But as I stood there, I began to feel distressed, and I said, "Somebody is lost in the river!"

My agitation grew, and I strained to see beyond a turn in the river. Then it seemed several people were just a few yards to my left, but I could not actually see them. I heard their voices saying to me, "They're not lost. They're just on up ahead but you can't see them right now. You can't be with them yet."

But then I became fully aware it was Ryan who was lost, and I jumped into the river, frantic in my efforts to find my son. The water was so very cold, but I pushed forward. Then, in a moment, I saw that I was surrounded by beautiful little fish of so many colors, oranges, yellows and reds. They were before me, behind me, over me and beneath me. I physically felt them propel me ahead, and as I traveled upriver, I said, "Oh, I didn't know how beautiful it was here! I didn't know how beautiful it was here!"

I did not get to the point of reaching Ryan, but my distress began to diminish. Then I awoke, almost feeling that I was still in the presence of the brightly colored fish that had guided me. It gave me a bit of comfort when I thought about them. The next day, I remembered that the fish is known as a symbol of Jesus, and they had been leading me to the place Ryan had gone.

I didn't know how we could possibly make it through Ryan's funeral. We were grateful that a dear friend named Michael, but also known as Chap, led the service, and he helped us make it a loving tribute. He recalled how Ryan would play at his house with his, Chap's, own son when both boys were little. He told how everyone he had talked to mentioned Ryan's love for and devotion to his children. And then how willing Ryan was to do anything for us, his parents, including climbing high on the roof of our two-story house to reach down and paint the peak there just below the overhang, even though he was afraid of heights.

My husband and I looked at each other and nodded and smiled when Chap said he had always felt Ryan was like a shy cowboy, who, when thanked for any small thing he had done, would shuffle his feet and say, "Oh, t'weren't nothin', Ma'am." It was so sweet to know that someone other than his obviously biased parents saw Ryan that way.

Chapter 13

Loss

It was unacceptable. That was the only way I could think of it. We were all grieving for Ryan—his father, his children, his siblings and his friends. I knew this, but for a long time I could only acknowledge my own grief. When I did think about how my husband was hurting and how Ryan's children had been robbed of the man they loved most, my hurt only became worse. My pain and my anger seemed burning hot, because this was so wrong.

In those first weeks, I know I was being somewhat shielded with the prayers of so many friends. But there was a point when I began pleading with God, saying "I know Ryan is in Heaven with You, but I just can't PICTURE it."

A mother has an innate, overpowering need to know that her children are safe. I repeated that plea, to be able to see Ryan somewhere safe, over and over, for two days. The evening of the second day, I was searching for a certain photo album I had not been able to find when we were getting pictures together for a memorial. I wanted to look at more pictures of Ryan. Behind a bookcase, where it must have dropped at one time, I found an old scrapbook. It was filled with things my children had made through the years. I turned the pages, and then I discovered why God had directed me to the scrapbook that day. It was so I could have my PICTURE. There was a drawing Ryan had made when he was in second grade. It showed a small boy standing inside the palm of a huge hand. There were clouds around the hand, a child's way of portraying Heaven. In careful, second-grade printing, Ryan had labeled the drawing, "Me in God's hand."

Several years later, I was in Los Angeles for a meeting. When I entered my high-rise hotel room, I wasn't quite sure what to make of the sculpture of a palm-upraised hand that was sitting on a small credenza. Perhaps it was a copy of a famous work, I don't know, but I felt it really wasn't my style. I just knew that it elicited a small, slightly odd feeling inside me.

I went out to do a little sightseeing, then came back to get ready to meet with some friends for dinner. As I left the room at 5:30, I took another look at the sculpture. I imagined I could be pictured with a puzzled look on my face, a little question mark in a cartoon balloon floating over my head. But then it was off to a pleasant evening.

The next morning, before I even opened my eyes, I was all too aware of the date, October 13th, the anniversary of the day of Ryan's attack that took him from us. After I dressed for the day, I paused at the sculpture of the hand on my way out. I tried to puzzle it out, why this large hand was affecting me so oddly. The realization brought on sudden tears as I finally understood why I had found myself in that hotel room with this curious up-raised hand sculpture. On this sad anniversary day, God wanted once more to remind me of the little boy who had drawn himself in the palm of his Father's hand.

I know God was holding me in His hand in the weeks and months following Ryan's death. I was thankful for the gracious little gifts He sent me, those assurances that Ryan was all right. But many times, I just wasn't able to stop and listen to His voice. Most of the time, I was drowning in grief. *It can't be. This isn't real. I can't accept this*, were the words constantly circling inside my head. I cried. I didn't know it was physically possible for a person to produce that many tears, day after day, after day.

We really didn't want to see people much. My husband would ask me to go out to lunch with him, and we began making a habit of going someplace in the small town next to us, with less likelihood of running into anyone we knew. Even at that, I think I cried all the way there every time and we would have to stay in the parking lot until I could pull myself together.

Sometimes I think my husband had to hold himself together so that his grieving wouldn't provoke more tears from me. He knew how I was feeling; I knew how he was hurting, but spoken words just couldn't convey it. We had to share our grief, mostly, in understanding silence. My husband lost his precious son, his companion and buddy, the one he could count on at some point almost every day, to come through the door, sit down and talk with him as they shared sections of the day's newspaper.

So, I am not saying his loss was any less than mine. But, I do believe that a mother's grief is more physical. When I was in public, I felt surprised that people weren't turning away from me in shock. I thought they must surely see the huge hole that I felt had been cut out of my body. Couldn't they see the anguish that was pouring like liquid from that jagged hole that had been torn in my chest? I know this sounds as though maybe I was going over the edge in my grief, but I think it was kind of a natural reaction. It had been years since I had held my son close, and even many more since I had carried him inside me. But I think a mother always carries an awareness of when she tenderly held her babies. She also cherishes the hugs of an older or grown child, and now the possibility of even holding my child's hand again had been stolen from me. *Not fair, not fair,* were the words now added to the loop of phrases running in my head.

It was either my stubbornness, or God's grace, that kept me on this side of sanity. For one thing, in the beginning I heard people talk about how this was "going to kill" me. Someone said I was going to end up in the hospital. Just like on that first night, when I made myself stop screaming into my pillow to avoid bringing on an HAE attack, I knew I couldn't let myself go too far. I didn't want to prove those people right. In the worst circumstances of my life, I had to be strong.

Eventually, people would say to me, "Ryan would want you to be happy. He wouldn't want you to grieve forever." I might have nodded at that, but inside I was thinking that the real reason I couldn't grieve too publicly was that Ryan would be saying, "Oh, Mom, stop, you're embarrassing me!"

He, the shy cowboy type, as Chap had said, never wanted attention drawn to himself. So, I behaved myself, most of the time. I also knew it would be so wrong if I turned all my focus away from the rest of my family. I wanted my other two children to know that I loved them and that they were just as important to me as Ryan was. I wanted my grandchildren to know that I would still be there for them. It wasn't easy. Once, as we were crossing a highway while driving to one of those lunch dates, I saw an oncoming semi in the lane we were crossing. Of course, there was enough time for us to get out of the way, but inside I was secretly saying, *Hit me. Hit me.* I knew that was wrong and I felt a little ashamed, but it was so hard to care, for a long time.

If I didn't know how I could go on, I certainly didn't know how I could celebrate the upcoming holidays after Ryan's death. Like many people do, I had a collection of light-up village houses that I enjoyed putting out at Christmas. I had collected them for many years, so it was a big project to set up my Christmas town, and it became a tradition for Ryan and me to work on it together. He was good at deciding which house should go where, and good at managing the cords, reaching places that I couldn't, in order to have them out of sight. As a mom, I was thrilled that my grown up son still enjoyed doing things with me. But that year, I knew I would definitely not be getting out my village houses, and probably never would again.

Then, in late October, Ryan's ex-wife, Laura, gave me a wrapped package. She told me it was something Ryan had gotten and planned to give me for Christmas. It had been in his closet. It was long and rectangular, and I was convinced it contained some kind of village house set. I felt so many emotions! I didn't think I could open something from him on Christmas morning. I believe I looked at that package every day for about a week, wanting to look, but not wanting to look. I finally decided the best thing to do would be to open it on Ryan's birthday, November 25th.

I felt it would be a small connection to him on that day, and maybe if it did contain village houses or accessories, that would be my sign to go ahead and continue the tradition, even though it would be hard. His birthday happened to be exactly six weeks after he died. I opened the package. Inside was a blue and white plaster Christmas train with little snow bears climbing on and hanging out the windows. I would not have to put out Christmas houses!

This was a treasured gift to me. That year I began using snowmen, because the little bears on the train looked like snowmen, instead of Christmas houses. They became my winter tradition, and the snowy train always took a place of honor among them. I always smile and thank

Ryan for this new way of welcoming the winter season.

People have asked us, "How can you stay in your house after what happened there, on your front porch?" This question always surprises me. Why would we want to leave this house we love, where we raised our children?

Of course, we have terrible memories of what happened that early morning, but one other thing occurs to me. It was tragic; we were frantic seeing what was happening to our son. But I am absolutely certain that when Ryan's heart stopped, there were angels hovering just above him. I don't really know what he was experiencing, but I believe it was something quite different than what we were feeling.

During that first winter, and many times after, I would go to the porch and sit on the steps, usually after dark so no one would see me. Maybe I would spend the time crying, but I also felt close to Ryan there. My husband and I like to sit on the front porch swing, talking, enjoying the breeze or a warm rain. Sometimes it does bring pain when we think of what happened there, but it is a part of our life's story. We never want to shut Ryan out of our memories.

Chapter 14

Blue, Blue Water

Ten months after Ryan died, I did something I'm still not sure was right. I went to Hawaii. I had my reasons. Our family had suffered another loss besides Ryan in the Fall of 2008. That Labor Day weekend we learned that my sister, Janet, had cancer. She died two and a half weeks later. My mourning for my sister was overshadowed, nearly wiped out, when, three weeks after her death, I lost my son.

The thing is, I had started to make plans to have as many far-flung family members as possible, to gather in Indiana for Thanksgiving. At the beginning of September, the idea that Thanksgiving would be too late did not occur to me in the least.

Janet and her family lived 500 miles away. We did make visits to her, but the three of us sisters, Janet, Toni and myself, always talked about meeting in the middle somewhere for a sister reunion. We had great ideas, but we didn't follow through. So, we finally had our reunion, but it took place around Janet's hospital bed in Little Rock, with her barely able to communicate with us. I returned home to Indiana, but ten days later, I had to travel back to Arkansas for her funeral. Our very last three sister reunion was at a quiet service, on a sunny day in an outdoor pavilion, with bees buzzing around Janet's memorial flowers.

Of course, on that September day, my biggest heartache was yet to come, and then I spent the following months in a grieving mother's haze. When spring came, my heart was still horribly broken, but I remembered the sisters' unkept promises, our unfulfilled resolutions. Toni and I talked, and we began to plan a trip for the coming summer. We decided we could manage a great sister adventure, an inter-island cruise in Hawaii. I wasn't sure how my husband would feel about this grand plan, but one day shortly after I told him, I came home to find a fresh pineapple on our mantel, along with a Bon Voyage card. So, we were set.

I don't know exactly when it started, but for many years I had dreamed of blue water. The dream usually involved a group of friends and myself on a trip somewhere tropical, and it was the last day and I would be telling the others we had missed the best part. It seemed my companions always wanted to stay in the hotel or go shopping and we hadn't even gone out to walk on the beach. We had wasted our time and I tried to tell them we were going to miss our chance to see the amazing white waves breaking out there in the incredible blue sea. Other times I would dream of gracefully swimming in that tantalizing, azure water. In those dreams, I was able to live, for a short while, in my colorful, lost world. At other times, my dream would be that I was at the ocean alone, trying to photograph the beautiful scene, and my camera wasn't working, or I had left it at home. That idea is anxiety-producing for me in real life since I so love to take pictures, and I felt the same anxiety in my dreams.

I think the sense of frustration and missing out in those dreams was an expression of that lifelong pursuit of my memory of colors. Or, it's possible that my dreams were trying to tell me I wasn't taking the time myself to appreciate all that God had given us to enjoy.

I have since been blessed with many chances to walk along beaches and photograph beautiful ocean scenes, and I am thankful for those times. But I feel that our Hawaiian cruise was a special gift. From the deck of the ship I could look out and soak up the gorgeous hues of the water. As we neared an island that would be one of our port stops, the juxtaposition of the royal blue of the water and the lush green of the land looked like Paradise to me. I have a photograph of one of those arrivals, with the ship's American flag proudly standing in the line of vision, adding its bright patriotic colors to the scene.

My sister and I rented a car so we could explore the island of Kauai. We saw amazing vistas, we stopped at state beaches and even swam a little, just to say that we had. Of course, at times on our trip, I sat on the beach or in a deck chair and cried. I certainly never forgot for a moment that I had lost my son, but Toni and I will always treasure our sister trip. At least, in this instance, we have memories instead of regrets.

Chapter 15

Bright Yellow Angels

Maybe my friend Thomas from the barn by the Ohio River and Joanne in the small plane in the storm weren't angels, but I believe God does sometimes send us special messengers when we need encouragement. It's His nature to want to do that for us, and for me, the beautiful little bird, the goldfinch, has often been the carrier of His messages. For many years, goldfinches have come along just when I needed lifting up the most.

It began one day when I was taking a walk in the country. I had hoped walking would help me ward off the looming presence of my familiar old depression. However, that day, not even the puffy white clouds in the blue summer sky or the sight of the lush fields were raising my spirit. But then, I looked up just in time to see the jerky, up and down flight of a pair of goldfinches crossing my path. They made me laugh out loud, and my mood rose watching them.

There have been many times since, when a goldfinch has flitted by just when I was sinking low. I remember a time lying in the chaise lounge in my backyard, looking up at the clouds and trying to pray away the negative thoughts that were plaguing me. My backyard has never attracted songbirds, because children have loudly played in the sandbox and on the slide through the years, and I could never hang bird feeders there since I didn't want to provide my cats with a free lunch. But I spotted a goldfinch playing in the trees above me that day, and I felt God wanted me to recognize it as His special sign.

It seems that it was His plan to continue this particular blessing. In 2012, I accompanied my father's 93-year old cousin to Disney World. Yes, Disney World! Betty loved Disney World. She had even been to Euro Disney in France. I had been hired to be Betty's traveling companion, but her two daughters were also along on the trip and we took turns pushing her wheelchair through the parks, so I had some time to myself.

I happened to be on a boat ride alone when some discomfort in my throat made me feel that it was beginning to swell. I leaned my head back on the seat, trying not to be afraid, but my runaway imagination soon gained ground. Was it getting worse? Would I be able to get off the ride and reach my rescue medicine in time? The ride seemed to go on and on, and the creeping fear was starting to give my limbs that weak feeling. Then began the familiar sensation of ice water running through my veins. I was heading toward a panic attack. I think I remembered my faith just in time. At the start of our trip, hadn't we all prayed for safety? So, why was I panicking? I did thank God for reminding me of His protection, and soon the tight feeling in my throat started to ease up.

The ride ended, and I got out of the boat and started walking away, my head hanging a little with shame and embarrassment for my burst of fear. As I was approaching an area of green, leafy trees, a fast, yellow blur shot across in front of me. I saw some movement in the trees; a lot of yellow blobs seemed to be jumping from limb to limb. Then I realized–they were goldfinches! There were at least a hundred of them, fluttering back and forth between the trees that lined both sides of the path. Of course, I grabbed my camera and took as many pictures as I could. The little birds allowed me to come close. As I reached in between the leaves, some of them brushed against my arm. God had given me goldfinches again. I believe He arranged my encounter with these little, yellow and black birds just to remind me that He is always with me, in spite of my doubts and fears.

I have always been thankful that God uses this pretty little bird, sometimes in an amazing way, when He sees me in spiritual or emotional need. One Sunday I was enjoying the worship service at church. But, as so often happened, it was hard to completely lay down my grief. I asked God, "Can You please help me to focus on the joy of knowing Ryan is in Heaven with You, rather than this pain of not having him here?"

The week had been hard, with my husband's and my grandson's and my birthdays all coming that very weekend. Ryan's presence was very much missed. Everything was different now; our grandson was even living four states away. Several days after that Sunday morning in church, I was still feeling very down and having trouble thinking about any joy. I decided to go to the cemetery to water the flowers I had planted the week before. A sad visit, until I saw what was lying on the base of Ryan's headstone: a tiny, yellow and gray goldfinch feather.

Chapter 16

Our Boy Moves East

Jeremy, our youngest child, had headed east after college, and he became a New Englander. Yes, he even became a Patriots fan! I have to forgive him for that, though, because he's also a Red Sox fan and he treated me to a memorable evening at Fenway Park a year or so ago. And there I got to fulfill a long-time desire to sing *Sweet Caroline* along with about 35,000 other fans.

After being in New England for several years, Jeremy met his future wife, the lovely Kate, at his job in Dover, New Hampshire. I was so excited the moment I met her, because I could tell she was the one for him. Her mother and I later compared notes and she laughed when I reported that Jeremy's first full sentence had been, "No, me do it." She said Kate's had been very similar!

The wedding was such a good thing for our family. Not only because we were happy for Jeremy and Kate, but also because in the sad years after losing Ryan, joyous occasions were not too numerous. I had so much fun choosing my mother of the groom outfit. My husband bought a nice-looking suit, paired it with a conservative gray dress shirt, and then picked out what I thought was an outlandish-looking necktie! I was worried that people would think it was a bit gaudy for a wedding. A lot of my friends had a similar opinion of the tie; my friend, Melissa, even suggested I might "accidentally" lose it out the car window on our drive to New Hampshire. But, I guess my fashion sense was too outdated, because when I sent Kate a picture of the tie, she thought it was just fine. I must say we all looked quite classy that evening, and the two photos of Jeremy tightly hugging first his father and then me, at the start of the ceremony, will be a treasure to us forever.

It was God's grace that got me through any anxieties and worries about traveling to Jeremy's wedding. The logistics for getting everyone where they needed to be were quite complicated, since my husband and I had obligations to be in two different places just two days after the wedding. We sorted it out, and got on the road, with Darrell and Jay doing most of the driving.

I had to keep my Mother Hen concerns to myself. Jay had only his learner's permit at the time and he had very little experience driving on interstates. He was probably wishing I could have been half-sedated, the way I had been that day Kristin had chauffeured me from my doctor's appointment. I made myself stay quiet in the back seat, and he did do a good job. But I couldn't quite let go of all my worry, since, because of our separate plans, just Jay and my husband would be making the drive home at the end of the week. I could imagine Jay driving on the interstate, my husband sleeping in the passenger seat, of course, without me there in the back seat to watch, and pray, and offer, at least mentally, my little bits of wisdom and safe driving tips. I truly tried to leave all of this in God's hands.

We arrived at Jeremy's house safely and had a wonderful weekend. Kristin and her husband and their youngest daughter, Anna, had made the trip from where they lived in Virginia. On the evening before the wedding, Kristin, Anna, and I ventured out in Kristin's car. We couldn't sit around in our hotel when we were so close to the coast of Maine. We bumbled around on country roads a little, but we finally found the coast.

We oohed and aahed at the foamy, crashing waves at several stopping points, and then we continued down the shore in hopes of finding the Nubble Lighthouse at the town of York. We did reach the lighthouse, but dark had fallen by then, and we could barely see the quaint, old structure. Everything was so dark, except for the intermittent flashing of the signal light that was revolving high above. We walked up close to the lighthouse, as did several other visitors, but we couldn't see much except rocks and water. Still, we were enjoying sharing this experience on that warm, breezy summer night. We walked back to the car and, raising our faces to the sky, we saw the beautiful gift that being there in the dark little village had bestowed upon us. We could see stars from one end of the sky to the other. Right above us stretched the Milky Way. It's a treasured memory we will always have, just because we had slipped away from the hotel that evening.

The day after the wedding, my husband and Jay and I needed to make our way down to Philadelphia, where Darrell was to attend a convention for five days. Jay was going to stay with him, and I was scheduled to fly to California the next day for a meeting of my own. We left New Hampshire with me in the driver's seat, my one condition being that Darrell take over the driving before we hit New York City. He agreed and on we went.

Those turnpikes tend to lull you along, and it seemed there were limited chances to get off to change drivers. Still, he assured me we would. We waited too long, however, because soon I found myself doing the one thing I hadn't wanted to do, drive through the great metropolis of New York City. I just wanted to stop in the middle of traffic and jump out and run around to the passenger side. But, those eighteen-wheelers and limousines and taxis were not going to let me do that. When I saw before me a huge, double-decker bridge and realized I had no choice but to drive across it, I very nearly closed my eyes to do so, but better judgment won out. I made it across. My protective angels must have been surrounding the car, something I appreciate, but I have no desire to repeat that experience.

Darrell made it to his meetings and I made it to my destination, Fresno, California. I enjoyed three days there, since I had made plans to stay with my HAE friend, Lois. She made it extra fun by driving me to Monterey so I could dip my toes in the Pacific, and be able to say I had been in both the

Atlantic and the Pacific in the space of three days. When my work and my visit were over, I flew home.

Of course, my car was not waiting for me at the airport, so I rented a car to get home. I was actually inside my county line when blue and red flashing lights filled my rear-view mirror. When I had pulled over, the officer asked me if I was aware I had a burned-out taillight. He was very understanding when I told him the car was a rental I had just picked up at the airport, and he let me go on my way.

I thought it was a little amusing though, that I had safely traveled coast to coast, visited nine states and two oceans, only to be stopped by an Indiana police officer ten minutes from my home. God's protection had been with us all again.

Chapter 17

New Treatments

People in the United States HAE community were rejoicing. A treatment that replaced the missing protein in our blood, successfully used in other countries for decades, had finally gained approval of the FDA. Some patients had received the treatment during trials for the drug, but now, any patient in the United States could potentially have access to it.

I had been looking forward to this happy day, of course, but as it turned out, the timing was terrible for our family. News of the FDA's approval came the very weekend Ryan suffered his laryngeal attack, with, of course, no supply of this life-saving medication available.

My reaction was to withdraw from most of my HAE friends. They all would have done anything for me, but at the time I just couldn't join in all the excitement about the newly approved medication. So, I mostly stayed offline, out of their discussion groups. My doctor was eager to have me try the new therapy, but I even shut her out for quite a while.

How could I take advantage of this life-changing and lifesaving treatment, when it hadn't been there for Ryan when he needed it? I was thankful for it, because it would help Kristin, her daughter who also had HAE, and two of Ryan's children who had HAE. That was the only bright spot in the situation. Kristin and these grandchildren were the future; they were stepping into a whole new world of possibility for HAE patients, but in those days, I still wasn't sure I even wanted a future for myself.

It was in preparation for my sister trip to Hawaii that I finally asked my doctor about prescribing the preventative medicine that had been on the market for nearly a year. I knew that starting on the therapy could help me avoid any possible emergencies on the trip, but there were other factors that finally made me decide to start it. I was still having bad HAE attacks at that time, and some were affecting my throat. Like so many of my friends who had this disorder, I spent nights wondering if I should go to sleep and risk that little tickle in my throat developing into a major swell and closing my airway.

I was just so tired of the whole thing. How many more urgent trips to the ER could I endure? I once went in for a badly swollen tongue and the doctor, not believing there was a serious problem, said, "But I don't know what your tongue normally looks like."

Finally, I thought of how it would only frighten my grandchildren if I, too, died of this terrible condition. I knew I needed to take care of myself, plus, I reasoned, I did need to get back to supporting the quest for new therapies. I needed to do all I could to make sure this and any other new treatments could thrive and be an option for my daughter and my grandchildren.

The newly approved treatment consisted of human-derived plasma containing the C1-inhibitor HAE patients need. It was to be administered by IV infusion. Patients would receive the medication, usually 10,000 units, in a simple procedure that took about ten minutes. Some patients needed the infusion twice a week, some less often and some more often, to keep a sufficient amount of C1-inhibitor in their system.

In the beginning, I had to go to an infusion center at our local hospital. With all the mixed emotions already working in me, it was very difficult returning to the place where our family's horrible heartache had played out the year before. I give credit to those nurses who helped me, twice a week at that time, who were so kind and understanding, telling me it was perfectly natural that I was crying in that place as I received my infusions.

Later, we obtained home health nursing service and I met many kind nurses through that, too. They even taught me to infuse myself. I was surprised it didn't bother me at all to put the needle into my arm or the top of my hand. I could easily find a vein, but so many times the vein would roll or blow out altogether and I would get frustrated. I do know how to infuse myself, but I still prefer my home nurse to do it for me.

One of my granddaughters does administer her own infusions. This is great for her, and I am happy there are even more options becoming available to treat acute attacks as well as preventative therapies that help keep attacks at bay.

Chapter 18

Maybe It's Time

If I had to survey all my faults, and that's a painful task for anyone, a big one would be judging people. I don't mean I go out and tell everyone what I think is wrong with them. It's just that, too often, I form a quick judgment in my mind over some little thing, whether it's any of my business or not. I'm not even so much referring to specific people. It more often concerns things that I might see in general that just don't match up to what I think is proper. Yes, again, as if it were my business. Sometimes, though, being judgmental can come back around to test you.

As an example, when I was a young mother and would see a magazine article in which a mother tells about losing her child, and it would show the mother with a pleasant smile on her face, yes, my judgmental thoughts would kick in.

How can she be smiling? I would think. Of course, *How dare she allow herself to smile?* was what I was really thinking. I truly didn't see how a parent could have any kind of life after losing a child, or even suggest there could be something to smile about.

Those mothers and fathers who went out and worked for a cause, maybe even created a foundation in a child's memory, were very admirable in my mind, but I didn't see myself as one who could do that. A year after Ryan died, about the time I decided to try the new medication, I experienced a little spark that showed me what might possibly lie ahead for me and my grief.

Several other drugs to treat Hereditary Angioedema were in the testing stages. I was asked to go a meeting in New Jersey and be part of a focus group, where we would learn about a particular treatment as well as share our own experiences with HAE.

As we sat around a long conference table, everyone's stories were, as usual, truly resonating with each other. In my mind, I was thinking I wouldn't even talk about Ryan. I thought I would feel more comfortable just telling them my thoughts on this new drug.

Then, a pretty, young mother from Georgia spoke. She said she was hesitant to treat a lot of her attacks, usually hoping they would go away on their own. When I heard her minimizing the throat attacks she had, I felt my body tense up. Even the person next to me, my good friend Marsha, noticed, and she gently rubbed her hand across my clenched hand in support. I couldn't decide if I should say anything.

It is true I don't normally have any doubts; I go ahead and share what I believe needs to be heard. But though I was hesitant back then, I did decide to speak up. I told the young woman, and all at the table, that I didn't want to frighten anyone, but ignoring some swelling in his throat very likely cost my son his life one year before. At the time, I hoped they didn't think I was being pushy or bossy, but, in many faces, I could see that my statement had struck a chord.

Maybe telling Ryan's story could help people.

A few more years went by. I still didn't want to have much to do with the HAE community. As before, though, I knew I should try to advocate for awareness, for new therapies, or for anything that would help my other family members handle their own HAE experience. I began to try to get involved with other patients once again.

One friend, Lora, holds some type of special event every year, in memory of her daughter, Lyndon, who passed away at age 12 from a laryngeal attack. It's a celebration of Lyndon's life, but also a way to spread much-needed knowledge about this terrible disorder.

When I decided to attend one of these events, which was a memorial walk, I knew it was going to be emotional. It was held in a nice city park, with a large picnic pavilion where everyone could come together. Two tables in the front were dedicated to pictures and mementos of people we had lost to HAE. I had supplied Lora with a picture of Ryan. He is sitting on our front porch swing, with his attention focused on his sweet little daughter who is wearing a silly headband with antenna-like balls standing out from it. It was Ryan at his happiest, spending time with one of his children. At the walk, it was so hard seeing Ryan included in that line of photographs, but it was a touching way to remember the many that we have lost.

It would take a whole book to write about Jenny, another mother whose son's picture was on the table that day. I'll just say, no one ever forgets Jenny. She is full of love and enthusiasm, and, as the saying goes, she has a mouth and she's not afraid to use it! Especially not at an HAE event, if it means somebody can learn or somebody can be helped. She dispenses her wisdom with her special gift of humor and wit, and always delivered in her memorable North Carolina accent.

At this memorial walk, Jenny and others were singing karaoke to entertain those at and around the pavilion. Jenny and I had already been friends since the early years, when we worked together toward raising HAE awareness and getting new medications approved. Then, it happened that Jenny's son died the same year as my son, exactly four months before Ryan. With that connection, our friendship moved on to an even deeper level.

So, I shouldn't have been surprised when Jenny rounded me up that day and said we needed to do a duet together. "There is no way," of course, was my first response. She badgered and cajoled a bit, until I agreed to look at the large book of song choices. On about my third turn of a page, there was a song that only the week before had made me think how appropriate the words were for Ryan and the way that he had to leave us.

"Okay, Jenny." I pointed to Vince Gill's *Go Rest High on That Mountain.*

"Yes," she answered, "let's sing it for our boys."

We started the song with Jenny being the brave one and prodding me along. I believe the crowd enjoyed our song, but Jenny and I soon found out for whom this little karaoke performance was really meant. It was for our boys, our babies, as Jenny had said when we introduced the song, but also for us as moms, who had so needed a way to express our loss and love.

Attending the picnic that day was a film producer, an HAE patient herself, who was making a documentary about HAE. Natalie had done a short interview with me, and I knew that it might be included in the movie. But while Jenny and I were singing, the film crew came forward and trained their cameras on us. We just went on singing; we were lost in our own world.

So then, it was a happy surprise, and an honor for us, when we found our tribute to our sons had become a small part of the documentary. The stories of Lyndon, Jenny's Jim, Ryan and others have since touched people all over the world with Natalie's movie, *Special Blood.*

Chapter 19

Advocating Once Again

Since HAE is such a rare disease, a big problem is many doctors don't understand it, or barely recognize the name. They might have read one or two pages about it in medical school ten or twenty years ago. I have heard more than one patient tell of explaining to a doctor, "I have Hereditary Angioedema," only to be dismissed by the doctor responding with some variation of, "Oh, you can't have that. It's too rare. Nobody has that."

This lack of knowledge would be frustrating enough to any patient trying to discuss his or her medical background; imagine the distress of someone having unexplained symptoms and going from one specialist to another, searching for answers. Most doctors don't even think of checking for HAE.

Many patients have had exploratory surgery, or even had healthy gall bladders or appendices removed, because their doctor did not recognize the signs of an HAE abdominal attack. So many patients tell of being left in the dark for so many years. The average time from onset of symptoms to being diagnosed used to be more than ten, possibly fifteen, years. However, that amount of time is beginning to decrease, thanks to the many more avenues for spreading awareness.

Groups such as the Hereditary Angioedema Association are constantly pursuing new ways to place accurate information into the hands of health care professionals everywhere. Their hope is to see the day when any health care provider, whether family physician, dentist, school nurse or emergency room personnel, will not have to say, "HAE? What is that?"

Of course, besides the medical community, HAE patients themselves, and their families, need to be educated. A person newly diagnosed, or even one who has been handling attacks alone for years, can feel that he or she is the only person in the world with this confusing disorder. So, when I had some opportunities to tell about my own HAE journey, I was excited to think of the people I might meet, and the things we might share with each other.

Just as in that focus group meeting in 2009, I immediately saw a response from people with whom I shared my family's story. Sadly, my family medical history with this condition goes back many generations, so I had quite a lot to tell when I spoke to small gatherings of patients.

I had a cousin, only 20 years old, who died of a laryngeal swell, while he was waiting for a cab to take him to the hospital. My mother's brother also passed away from HAE at a young age. And then, from studying genealogy and piecing together family history, we learned that tragic HAE deaths had occurred in at least two earlier generations. My great-grandfather's obituary calls his death "a strange demise" due to "strangulation." Obituary notices were much more detailed back then, the early 1900s. My great-grandfather's even tells how he came up to the house from working in one of his fields and asked for a glass of water, because he had an odd feeling in his throat. He then returned to his field, but did not come back when he was expected. A few men went out to look for him and found him on the ground, unable to communicate with them.

A doctor who was called diagnosed some sort of swelling around the larynx, but he did not know any more. The article continued to state my great-grandfather passed away in the doctor's arms. Then, several years later, my great-grandfather's daughter, my mother's mother, died of what was assumed to be the flu. Family lore said she seemed to be getting better, but then suddenly died and no one could understand why.

Since we know that HAE does not skip generations, my grandmother had to have had it in order to pass it down to my mother. So, it is very likely her death came during an HAE episode, rather than from a relapse of the flu. My mother was only one year old when she lost her mother.

It's true these sad reports touched people when they heard them, but I wasn't relating them for sympathy or just for the sake of story-telling. I wanted the patients to understand how dangerous and unpredictable HAE can be. The good thing is, my stories made an impact, and people I spoke with often told me they had a change in attitude about their own attacks, realizing that they needed to be taking their condition more seriously.

Of course, our talks were not only about what we have lost. The very fact of being with other people who understand, those who have "been there," is such a good experience for patients Talking together discussing all the options we now have to prevent and treat attacks encourages everyone. This is such a difference from the days of my childhood, when I watched my mother and my sister and my cousin suffer. They had no one they could talk to and gain any perspective.

I have enjoyed every bit of being able to advocate for HAE awareness. I love the people I meet and the places I go. But then, so many times, I hear from someone how wonderful they think it is that I'm sharing about my son. I always think to myself, *No, no, I'm not THAT mother!* It truly does bother me that I am doing something that yes, I love, but here I am talking about this horrible thing that took my son's life.

Do I really want to talk about Hereditary Angioedema and re-live all the pain and heartache the disease has brought to my family through so many generations? It sometimes makes me feel that I should go back into hiding, turn away from anything to do with HAE, other than doing my own treatments or helping my family members with theirs.

Then I will remember certain ones who have told me, "I understand how dangerous laryngeal swelling is now" or, "I am going to have my children tested now." And they have told me they will encourage siblings or cousins to talk to their doctors about their HAE. Just as I treated my diagnosis so nonchalantly when I was a teenager, I know that many people don't like to face the reality of living with a life-threatening condition. So, getting together and talking one on one can benefit patients and their loved ones, as well.

One event did show me that maybe I really was "that mother". Who would have thought that one day I would be telling my family's story on Capitol Hill in Washington, D.C.? I had the opportunity to participate in one of the HAE Association's visits to Washington. In groups of three or four, we met briefly with representatives from our respective communities. Our goal was to let them know how legislation and prospective bills would affect people with rare diseases like ours.

We were so grateful for new medications, but the problem remained, would all patients be able to access them? We respectfully asked our representatives to support bills that would make insurance coverage attainable for all. As well, we wanted them to take steps to insure that Hereditary Angioedema would remain on the list of rare diseases that receive federal funding for research. We were able to leave them with several pages of facts and figures relating to our causes, but more importantly, we had the opportunity to show them the human face of HAE.

We wanted them to realize that in their own constituency there were real people who were battling this real disease, and we needed our representatives in our corner. I had taken with me that day a copy of the photograph of Ryan and Thomas kicking a football on that beautiful October day in 2008. I shared the picture to show them what HAE had taken from us, and to explain why we were there: to do all that we could to see that these stories of loss would someday be a thing of the past. That was one day when I really felt good about telling Ryan's story, and I felt that maybe he was a little proud of me.

Whether it's been through events sponsored by the HAE Association, through online chats with other patients, or through my own advocating travels, I have gained so many friendships that will truly last a lifetime. That has to be better than shutting myself away and refusing to interact with others. When I do that, I am forfeiting my chance to have those very special give and take relationships.

Among the many wonderful HAE friends I have made, I have to count as precious a certain one, Ike, Ike the Service Dog. Something about his serious, dark, bearded face made me fall for him from the first pictures I viewed on Facebook. He belongs to a patient named Jennifer, and through the years she has reported his many loving acts of care and devotion. He goes with her everywhere. My first face to face meeting with Jennifer and Ike was at a dinner meeting in California. Two years later, we met again at a conference in Minnesota. There were so many people there that we were all busy, going from table to table, trying to catch up with everyone. I spent some time standing by Jennifer's table as we enjoyed a nice conversation. Then I became aware of something that seemed a little odd in that setting. I felt something on my foot, and I looked down to see Ike, resting his chin there, just drowsing contentedly. I felt like I was being blessed by a national hero!

Jennifer told me that since it's his job to be aware of all of her needs, Ike doesn't interact with, or warm up to a lot of people, and it was special that he did with me. It was an honor. Maybe I was being overly sentimental about it, but I treasured Ike's gesture of trust and friendship. Just like they do for people who have other disorders, service animals can alert an HAE patient to impending attacks, or simply be there for them when daily activities are difficult. This is just one more reason I say dogs are a gift from a loving God. He wants to supply every one of our needs.

Chapter 20

Grace on a Plane

Flight attendants who greet me as I step onto a plane might notice how I always first touch the side of the plane and say a quick few words, before looking up at them and returning their smile and hello. This might have started as a fear thing—*make sure you pray before getting on that huge metal thing that's going to lift you up 30,000 feet in the sky!*

Of course, anyone should pray and ask for protection before any endeavor, taking off through the clouds or not. But it became a natural habit for me to place my hand on the side of the aircraft door and quietly say, "Thank you Lord, for a safe trip, in Jesus' name." I don't use this as a good luck ritual; I am simply acknowledging that "God is my shield and protector" and thanking Him for it.

It's true I have been known to grab my seatmate's hand, whether I knew the person or not, when an uneventful flight has suddenly turned into a jerky, rocky ride. Mostly though, I stay cool and calm through little bumps and dips.

My cool, serene state was tested one day on a flight out of Minneapolis. We had been in the air about 20 minutes when everyone came to attention at the sound of a THUMP that seemed to be coming from the bottom of the plane. When no more sounds came, everyone looked around with little smiles of relief. Then, the captain came on the speaker—always a rather scary event in itself—and announced we really shouldn't worry, but he needed to tell us that the sound we had heard had come from the landing gear dropping down, obviously not when it should have been doing so.

He assured us they were going to remedy the problem. A little later, he told us they were trying to fix the landing gear remotely, from a computer on the ground, a procedure which we passengers had no clue of understanding, but, I believe we were all thinking, "All right, please do that."

So, we all sat and listened to the whirring of the landing apparatus as it went up, down, up again, and then down. The next announcement went something like, "Well, folks, we are sorry, but that just isn't working. We're going to turn around and head back to Minneapolis." He then went on to explain that they could not be sure the landing gear was completely extended in the way it would need to be. He told us, "We need to prepare for a crash landing." There were several gasps in the cabin, and now those faces that had offered the little smiles of relief were turning pale; fear was creeping in.

Still oddly calm, I checked my thoughts and emotions. I was still feeling serene. The surprise at this fact was enough to keep me occupied for a few minutes. We were given instructions: put everything away, put our heads between our knees, and once we land, do not make a move until we were told.

It was becoming more real now. People were praying. It's like a foxhole situation—everybody prays in a disabled aircraft. I was still experiencing this odd peace. I realized I wasn't praying, "Oh, please let us be all right." Instead, I was marveling at the fact that I believed I was going to be all right, no matter what happened. This was a huge revelation for the girl who had held on to so much fear and worries most of her life. God's grace at 30,000 feet.

I did say a prayer for those who seemed to be so fearful, that they would have this peace, also. We returned to Minneapolis, and as fire trucks and other emergency vehicles lined the landing strip, our airplane touched down with just a slightly rougher bump than normal. Everyone cheered, I'm sure there were some "Thank you, Jesus!" shouts offered up, also. I knew I had two things for which to be thankful, a safe, event-free landing, and God's gift of sweet reassurance right in the midst of a potentially tragic situation.

Chapter 21

Feelings

"How does that make you feel?" "I have feelings for him." "Feelin' good!"

We gauge the quality of our lives so much on how we feel. Even though the Bible tells us that we should walk by faith, not by sight, we are always wanting to check our feelings to see if we are heading in the right direction. But I know feelings can fool us. Just as there wasn't really a wolf in the dark living room the night I had that childhood fever, so many of my fearful moments truly held no danger. Our thoughts and emotions, and, as in the case of that fevered night, our body systems, can sometimes lie and try to make us believe things that aren't really there.

I am not discounting the power of emotions or the genuine torment of depression. They absolutely affect our life. No one that I know is immune to negative thoughts, or to letting external situations influence their feelings. But a little maturity, well, I should say *years* of maturity has left me with a somewhat new perspective.

The fact is, things are scary. Dark gray wolves, an unsure medical prognosis, and teenage drivers are scary. Misunderstandings between loved ones are scary. However, we usually get through them. They are the kinds of things that make up life, and most of the time, our feelings of fear and our worry were just a waste of time. They probably even took a toll on our health. I have certainly been through plenty of situations like that.

Besides the things that made me afraid or depressed, I have been blessed with a thousand "good feeling" moments. Like seeing my babies being born, and feeling exquisite love for these little persons I had known for nine months, but now was able to see and hold in my arms. And then, the births of my grandchildren, and the shock of love and adoration I instantly felt for each of them.

I have had great spiritual moments that "felt good". At an evangelist's meeting once, I experienced the presence of God so keenly that I wanted to stay there forever, basking in the tremendous love that seemed to be saturating my body. During a women's Bible study meeting, I had such a feeling of being protected and cared for when someone told me she had seen an angel standing at my side as I was sharing a difficult personal story. I think extraordinary moments like those truly are from God. He wants us to see Him and love Him more than we already do. Of course, the little times of joy are from Him, too. Hearing beautiful music, watching funny dogs play together, a wonderful meal, a warm summer rain are all things He takes pleasure in giving us.

I've probably given thanks a thousand times for those good feeling-inducing moments. It has just become a part of my every day to talk to God and tell Him I'm thankful for things, both big and small. I'm thankful for good, working, home appliances. I'm thankful when I'm merging on to an interstate and traffic is spaced out far enough that I can blend in without a hitch. But the change is, I've gradually learned to thank Him for His presence in the hard times, too.

I can remember one time, in recent years, lying on the bathroom floor during an HAE attack, desperately nauseated and crying with the pain. For some reason, this attack wasn't going away any time soon. I didn't stop hurting, and the nausea didn't let up, but this time, in spite of all these out of control symptoms, right there on the floor, I became aware of God's peace. I didn't have to "feel good" to believe God cared. I didn't even have to clean myself up in an attempt to become worthy. I was actually quite a mess, and my feelings were leaning towards a lot of self-pity and a little anger that I was having to endure this awful attack. But my pain and self-pity and giving into anger really didn't matter much that night. It seemed that God's grace came swooping in, calming me, as He let me know that He was so much bigger than my feelings, good or bad.

Maybe I was on to something.

What if it wasn't about me?

What if I had been trying to figure out God with my little, limited, human reasoning power? I sometimes fail people; my family sometimes fails people; my friends sometimes do. So, maybe I was mistaking God for someone who hadn't quite gotten this unconditional love thing down. Maybe I wasn't realizing that He's a big God and I'm a little me. And I didn't realize that that is actually a good thing.

I think about my babies. From the moment I knew them, I loved them with an astonishing love. As they grew, they sometimes tried my patience. They made messes, and they made mistakes. Not once did I decide I could not forgive them. Not once did I stop loving them. If I could be so generous in my, admittedly imperfect, love, why did I think God wasn't quite capable of loving me and forgiving me just as completely? God is about a billion times wiser, kinder, more patient, and more loving than I am. So, maybe I had better take Him at His word that He can take care of me, that He loves me, and that He will neither leave me nor forsake me.

Chapter 22

Living in Color

Was I just being a whiny little girl, back there in the days of sitting in my swing, yearning for something more? I really don't think so. There were several different things that probably allowed depression, doubts and fear to move into my little mind. The first thing might simply have been my physiology. Maybe, as well as the biological marker for brown eyes and the mutated gene for hereditary angioedema, I also received genes that set me up for depression and brooding introspection. Then these all came together with my other genes to make up the being called me.

Also, things that little ears hear can shape a child's life for years to come. My mother had a very rough time carrying me. For some reason, her friends seemed to like to remind me that she had been sick for nine straight months with me. Well, that is enough to plant a little guilt in a child. And then, the story goes, I cried for a solid year. What a great start I had. Also, I had to hear over and over how my grandmother, my father's mother, told my parents, "You'll never raise her." I did go on to be a reasonably healthy child, and I enjoyed lots of love and care, but who wants to hear her grandmother basically pronounce a death sentence over her?

Maybe it was there I made a wrong turn. I listened to those bad reports and took them too much to heart, weaving them into my still developing identity. It is no wonder then, when some common illness, or Hereditary Angioedema, threatened me, I feared the worst. I believed I would never get well, that there was no hope for me.

But where did my memory of color come from? Was that lovely, color-splashed world real? I'm not sure, but I have some ideas about it. I think it's always been God's plan for us to live healthily, happily and peaceably on this earth. Maybe we all start out with that ideal imprinted upon us. But then, it's obvious that God's beautiful earth has been tainted in a lot of ways, and His plan for us to live a perfect life in a perfect world has gone awry, too. Not saying He has failed; we humans have. We miss the mark over and over; we have not handled what we have been given as well as we could have. We have to be thankful, though, He doesn't give up on us and He always strives to bring us back to all the things He has wanted for us since the beginning.

If it is true what I heard from my mother's friends, that she was sick for nine months, and that I cried my whole first year, yes, it seems I got a rough start in life. Then, I went through a lot of common and also less common illnesses, compounded, of course by my depressive tendencies. But through it all, I was holding on to my belief that there was a hidden world of color somewhere, whether that was in my memory or in my heart's promise.

There is still deep pain in my heart. I miss Ryan every single day. I still think I should see him coming through the front door for a quick visit before going to work. Of course, I know that can't happen, but the mind plays little tricks on us. We know our loved one is gone, but in order to live day to day, we have to tuck that knowledge and our grief in a back corner of our mind. So many times, though, it comes back to me all at once. Every single time, it is a heart-rending shock to suddenly so clearly remember what happened to my son.

I have experienced many happy times since October of 2008. It didn't seem possible for that to happen, and it didn't seem right to me. How dare I enjoy something? I think the answer is the grace of God, and family. At first, I believe, God said, "You are going to go on, whether you want to or not."

Those little wishes for a truck to hit me or the even more morbid incident when I almost raised my hand to pick up a container of drain cleaner in the grocery store—well, those things didn't come to pass. I'm sure it was God saying "Nope, it's not your choice, not your time."

Of course, He was right. It would have been a terrible time for me give up and leave this life. How would my other two children have felt if I decided life wasn't worth living since I was missing the third? If I gave up the choice of seeing them in the here and now so I could go on and be with Ryan? I didn't want to do that to them; I couldn't do that to them. For that matter, how could I leave my husband alone? My grandchildren needed me, too.

Ryan's children had lost their father and Kristin's girls had lost an uncle they loved. In these years since 2008, I've watched these grandchildren grow, and have rejoiced over new tiny additions to the family. I would have missed so much.

As I write, my neighborhood, my town, and nearly half the country are lying under a blanket of crystalline, white snow. The temperature has been below zero most nights. But not too many weeks ago, my husband and I were strolling along streets and beaches in Colombia, South America, and Panama and Belize. Wow, did God open up a world of color for me there!

We visited an emerald museum. I have always loved this green stone. My husband could barely tear me away from the displays. Such beauty, such gorgeous riches from the Earth itself. I've never had many jewels, only my diamond engagement ring and a few other small stones. Although I had always admired the emerald, I never particularly dreamed of owning a lot of precious stones as some people do. But, oh, did my desire kick in that day in the emerald museum. I could almost say I was lusting over the many fine distinctions in the shades of those emeralds. I'll just say, I was enjoying very much what my eyes were beholding.

Besides the emeralds, I found myself appreciating and enjoying other stones on this trip, too. I saw stones in shades of blue I don't remember ever seeing before. Some were a deep, yet bright, color of blue that almost made my eyes hurt. And there was a stone of a milky medium blue that I found myself yearning to own. Of course, the price tags cut those yearnings short. That was all right; my eyes had feasted, and I was happy with my cubic zirconium palm tree ring that I bought as a memento of our trip.

Other fabulous colors dazzled us on this wonderful trip. The luscious yellow of a hibiscus hanging over us as we lunched at an open air restaurant on a beach in Colombia, and the sky blue of a butterfly's wings in a garden in Belize. I'll always remember the evening I got the perfect shot of the setting sun spilling a flood of amber diamonds across the waters of the Atlantic Ocean. And the evening we saw dusky blue clouds painted with large swaths of rosy color, reflections of that day's setting sun.

Maybe I was able to appreciate the colors because of the peace inside of me. God's grace has brought me through so much. It has brought my husband and me through so much since 2008. This trip was a wonderful gift to us, probably the best one we have ever had.

The emeralds and the other jewels I got a glimpse of and viewed with a newly appreciative eye? I don't have to have them on my hands or wrists or around my neck. God reminded me that Heaven's walls will be built of these very stones and I'll get to walk among them one day. For now, I am thankful for His grace, which has brought color back into my life, a new contentment back into our family and the assurance we ARE enough for Him. He loves us that much.

Made in the USA
Middletown, DE
31 March 2018